REFLECTIONS ON THE SYNOPTIC GOSPELS
AND THEIR SPECIAL DESIGN

Reflections on the

alba house ▪ DIVISION OF THE SOCIETY OF ST. PAUL
STATEN ISLAND, N.Y. 10314

Synoptic Gospels

and Their Special Design

Forbes J. Monaghan, S. J.

Imprimi Potest:
Robert A. Mitchell, S.J.
Provincial of the New York Province

Nihil Obstat:
Edward Higgins, O.F.M. Cap.
Censor Librorum

Imprimatur:
Joseph P. O'Brien, S.T.D.
Vicar General, Archdiocese of New York
February 4, 1970

The nihil obstat and imprimatur are official declarations that a book or pamphlet
is free of doctrinal or moral error. No implication is contained therein that those who
have granted the nihil obstat and imprimatur agree with the contents, opinions or
statements expressed.

Library of Congress Catalog Card Number: 70-110595
SBN: 8189-0171-3

Designed, printed and bound in the U.S.A. by the Pauline Fathers and Brothers of
the Society of St. Paul, 2187 Victory Blvd., Staten Island, N.Y. 10314 as part of their
communications apostolate.

CONTENTS

PART ONE: A FAREWELL TO JERUSALEM

PART TWO: TWO SAILED FROM PHILIPPI

IN MEMORY
of
MY BROTHER LEO
Priest and Jesuit
R. I. P.

INTRODUCTION

It is a sound rule that problems pertaining to a special field should be left to those who have been trained for that field. Scripture problems should be left to scripture specialists. That rule is violated by the present book. Its author is not a scripture specialist, and his work has imperfections that are inevitable when a general practitioner intrudes within the province of the specialist.

He can, however, plead an excuse for his intrusion. Problems on whose solution hang consequences of the gravest sort should be left to the specialists — till it is plain that the specialists will not solve them. When a man is drowning in the surf, his rescue should be left to the lifesavers. But if the lifesavers are on strike, and only one person on the beach (a scripture specialist, let us say) can swim a little, the responsibility for saving the drowning man devolves on him. He must not excuse himself. He must not argue, "This is not my métier. I am a scripture specialist, not a lifesaver." He must dash into the surf.

The present writer's responsibility did not arise in precisely that way. The scripture scholars have not gone on strike, nor have they overlooked the importance of the problem that is attacked in this book. If they were asked, they would doubtless reply that no more momentous question confronts them than that of the design of the first three gospels; that on its solution depends the security of Christian faith itself. Since the specialists have been toiling ceaselessly to solve it, how can there be a need for one not of their guild to attack it?

The need arises from this; that only one method of attacking the problem guarantees its solution, and this method the scripture specialists cannot be induced to use. When the whole fire department has thundered off down the wrong road and become lost, we should not rebuke a bucket brigade for taking the right road and fighting the flames in its amateurish way.

Such, figuratively speaking, was the situation that produced this book. The irony of the situation was that the scripture specialists themselves created the method that they cannot be induced to use.

They created it when they proved that our first and third gospels were built on the narrative found in our second. That proof (on which they justly pride themselves) was a triumph of scientific method. When Matthew and Luke were laid alongside Mark and compared with it, line by line, they were seen to agree with each other often and in much detail — but, with only a few exceptions, only when they agreed with Mark. It seemed impossible to explain why, if they had not used Mark, they agreed with each other so much when they also agreed with him; but agreed with each other so little when they disagreed with him.

Here was a breakthrough of the greatest importance in scripture studies: one that released the biblical specialist henceforth from relying on guesswork and hunch in determining the design of the synoptic gospels. For if it was certain that the authors of our first and third gospels used the Marcan narrative, every change they made in that narrative was intentional; it was an index of the author's design. This fact is the foundation on which the only safe and scientific method of ascertaining the special design of the synoptic gospels can be built.

The special design of a work reveals its author's special purpose: his concrete purpose, molded by the circumstances of the situation that impelled him to write.

He achieves this purpose by a series of choices, each of which is dictated by some detail of the purpose. Those choices deal with the contents of his composition: viewing the materials at his disposal in the light of their usefulness to his purpose, he selects this and rejects that. They also deal with the arrangement of his materials; with the relation between them that is dictated by his purpose. Suppose the materials to be but these two: "Jones is intelligent," and "Jones is immoral." He can write, "Jones is intelligent but immoral," and condemn Jones. Or he can write, "Jones is immoral but intelligent," and approve him.

At the end of his series of choices the writer rests. He has achieved the concrete purpose that impelled him to write. Every detail of it has been translated into a corresponding detail of his composition.

Paramount in importance among those details are the *differentiating* ones.

What impels an author to write is some *new* need. If the new features of this need were satisfied by some existing work known to him, he would not toil to produce a new work. Because they are not satisfied by any existing book, he must write a new one with features that differentiate it from existing books. The differentiating features of the book correspond to the differentiating features of the new need that impelled him to write. Hence, by analyzing those of the book we can discover those of the new need — and we can learn the distinctive features of the situation that created the need. Then, if we can identify this situation, we shall know where and when he wrote the book.

We can make such an analysis, however, only if we can lay the book side by side with the previous works which dealt with the same subject, and from which the author consciously departed. Till it was proved that the authors of our first and third gospels used Mark's narrative, we could not know whether their departures from it were intentional. We could not know, for instance, whether they omitted a Marcan incident because they did not know of it, or because they did not want it — it did not fit into their design. So, being in the dark on this essential point, the specialists could only guess, play hunches, let their feelings or prejudices select the Matthean or Lucan passages that unlocked for them the author's purpose and all that went with it. On a matter of gravest import to Christian faith they could give only insecure opinions; little systems that had their day and ceased to be.

Now, this embarrassment of the specialists ended when they proved that the authors of our first and third gospels used Mark's narrative. They knew for certain now that *all* the departures of those gospels from the second were intentional. They could now proceed scientifically to ascertain the special design of those gospels, using the same method that specialists in other fields employ to crack a code, decipher a strange language, or assemble the pieces of a puzzle in archeology or crime. That method we are going to use in this book. Its steps are as follows:

First, we eliminate the irrelevant data; those differentiating details, such as mannerisms and points of style, that are due not to a writer's purpose but to his personality. Of this sort, generally speaking, are the merely modal variations of Matthew and Luke from Mark; variations that say the same thing in different words. To sift these for hints of their author's purpose would be wasted time; whatever they can tell us we shall learn more quickly from the substantive variations.

We confine our study, then, to the substantive omissions, insertions, and rearrangements which the author of the first (or third) gospel made as he built on the Marcan narrative. Since his omissions tell us not what his purpose was, but what it was not, our main attention will be on his positive changes — his insertions and rearrangements of material. What we seek in them is *purposeful patterns*.

Variation X produces a certain effect. When variation Y produces the same effect, a pattern has emerged. If this pattern is repeated, if it combines with other patterns to form larger ones, we may be able to conclude that it was not accidental but intended. It is a *purposeful pattern*. By combining these purposeful patterns we can predict identical or complementary patterns in other areas of the gospel; and then verify the predictions. As we proceed thus from area to area, the shape of the writer's design will begin to loom through the haze. When the total evidence — that is to say, *all* the substantive variations — has been assessed in this way, that design should flash forth in every part of the gospel and proclaim its message.

Such was the instrument that the proved dependence of Matthew and Luke on Mark's narrative placed in the specialists' hands. Yet they seem unaware that it exists. When they discuss the purpose of the synoptic writers they stick to guesswork and hunch; giving us opinions endlessly various and mutually contradictory, each defended by a faggot of texts and demolished by another faggot. They have not begun to realize what the evidence is that they have to assess.

Most glaring, perhaps, is their neglect of the rearrangements of Marcan material made by the authors of our first and third gospel. One instance can be cited here out of dozens that will be studied in this book. It is the long section of Matthew extending from chapter 5 to the end of chapter 13. Outside this section the author regularly presents his Marcan materials in the Marcan order. Inside it he radically rearranges that order. The new arrangement is intentional, and little study is needed to show that his intention was not to give the incidents a more accurate chronology. Manifestly, that section conceals an important clue to the author's design. What does the scripture specialist do with it? He points to the rearrangement as an interesting phenomenon and passes on. He does the same with other Matthean rearrangements that are equally striking; some he does not even notice. This is a fatal oversight. In the arrangements of his material lurks the soul of the author's purpose; and whoever does not probe relentlessly to find the reason for them will not be able to tell what the purpose was, nor the circumstances that shaped it.

How it has happened that an able and zealous body of specialists, deservedly held in honor by the Christian world, have left unused this splendid tool which their own successful labors had put into their hands; why it is that they keep the question of the design of the synoptic gospels bogged down in guesswork and hunch, only they can say. The present writer simply points to the fact, which he believes they will not deny.

They will not deny that the method he has outlined above — the only method that takes into account the full evidence that must be considered — is the only one that can lead to secure conclusions. They will not deny that they have failed to use it. And if they are candid, they will probably not deny that they remain averse to using it even when it has been pointed out to them.

When they have made those admissions, they will not be intolerant in judging this book. As they cast up the score of its defects, they will bear in mind that its author spent years of no little toil on it because he saw devolve on him the responsibility that was theirs and that they did not shoulder.

Two kindly critics have warned the writer that the book will not be seriously considered by scripture scholars because it has few footnotes. It is hard to believe this. Those scholars have seriously considered — and adopted and made their own — all sorts of theories born of guesswork and hunch about the design of the synoptics. There is a theory in vogue among Catholic scholars about the design of Matthew. This theory, that of the Five Books, rests on one fact and one fiction. The fact is that Papias, a second-century bishop, wrote five books of commentary on Matthew's gospel. The fiction is that the gospel has five big discourses; whereas, in fact, it has six. After the scholars have swallowed such camels of indefensible theory, and the only study of synoptic design that has ever followed the right method of ascertaining that design comes along, would it not be anomalous for them to look down their nose at it because it does not come knee-deep in footnotes? Would this not be to put the first things last and the last things first in a quite unscriptural sense?

What, after all, would they want discussed in those multitudinous footnotes? The currently fashionable theories that are born of an essentially unreliable method and are therefore essentially unreliable? Once the essentially unreliability of those theories is conceded, they'll have been sufficiently discussed. The exposition, given above, of the method they had to follow and did not follow is all the footnote they require. Footnote and epitaph. Before we move on to the first chapter of this book, those theories are dated and dead. If this book fails in its enterprise, they will not get a new lease on life. The failure of this book would merely prove that the method it followed must wait for a sturdier pioneer than the present writer. For a scripture specialist, of course. May the imperfections of the book goad one of them to do the job himself and do it perfectly.

Some words now about the contents of the book. It has two parts. Part One deals with Matthew and Mark. Part Two deals with Luke's gospel and the Acts. The Acts could not be omitted, because its design is indivisible from the gospel's; they are parts of one plan.

Part One, in particular, will try the reader's patience and endurance. Let him hark back to the steps of the method we are going to employ, and he will see why. We shall have to study *all* the evidence: all the substantive Matthean variations from the Marcan story. We shall have to fit each piece of evidence into a web that relates it to every other piece, till they make one luminous message to which each piece contributes. We shall have to check each piece with this message. We shall have to check the message itself with what the earliest Christian tradition has reported about it. When the reader sees the entire evidence lie open, like a completed jig-saw puzzle, under his eyes; when he can verify for himself that the pieces are all present and accounted for, he will enjoy a greater security about the book's conclusions than inspired guesswork and hunch can give him; but he must pay a stiffer price for this security.

The conclusion we reach from our analysis of the first gospel is that it was designed as an apostle's farewell message to the church of Jerusalem. The conclusion we reach about the third gospel is that Luke designed it to show the agreement between Christ's teaching and the theology of Paul that we find in Romans and the epistles that preceded Romans.

While the book may give the impression of being top-heavy with argument, it has only three basic propositions. They are:

1. Every substantial departure from the Marcan narrative that is made by the author of our first or third gospel is an index of his design.

2. The second gospel records the instructions that Peter gave in Jerusalem between 30 and 42 A.D.

3. In the texture of the Acts there is a discontinuity that starts with the account of the riot at Ephesus.

The second of those propositions is just as important as the first. If it is solidly probable (the present writer believes it has more than probability), the supposedly impregnable case for the priority of Mark's gospel to Matthew's breaks down. With the collapse of that case the towering superstructures of biblical and theological speculation that have been erected on it must collapse too,

> And like an insubstantial pageant faded,
> Leave not a rack behind.

One prominent feature of the first gospel, the condemnation of the Jewish people by Christ and the apostles, is a sensitive subject these days. This condemnation, the writer has pointed out in a note, was limited to a single generation of the Jewish people and was aimed directly only at the Jewish leaders. He thinks, nevertheless, that something further should be said here about his personal feelings on this matter. His Jewish friendships have given him an insight into the deep, warm goodness of the Jewish people; an insight that is one of the fine experiences of his life. Because of it he wants to increase and strengthen the bridges between Christian and Jew. He trusts that his study of Matthew's special design will not weaken them. We can find an analogy to that design in the Declaration of Independence. As Jefferson dwelt with strong emotion on the reasons why the colonies had to break with Britain, so Matthew dwelt with strong emotion on the reasons why the apostles had to break with Israel. As Americans can and should read the

Declaration without letting its emotion toward the British government of 1776 bias them against the British people of today, so Christians can and should read Matthew's gospel without letting its emotions toward the Jewish govenment of 42 influence them against the Jewish people of today. Even to the "villains" of long ago we bear no animosity. Lord North and Caiaphas stir no wrath in us. Why then should they keep an American from admiring Englishmen or a Christian from liking Jews?

This introduction must not close without a brief, inadequate tribute of gratitude from the writer to Miss Ellen Murphy. He knows that without her devoted, persevering help this book would not have reached publication. He is grateful also to Alba House, his publisher, and to all the friends who gave their support to him in the years when he was working on the book.

PART ONE
A FAREWELL TO JERUSALEM

1

CALLED TO THE GENTILE WORLD

In our first gospel three areas particularly invite study. They are the resurrection story (27:62-28:20) with which it ends; the temple discourse of Holy Tuesday (21:23-23:39); and the section (4:23-13:58) that extends from the call of the first disciples to the death of John the Baptist. The ending of a work is or-dinarily the place where its design is completed; and Matthew's ending has unique features. The temple discourse is the emotional peak of the gospel; presumably, then, it is a focal point of the author's interest. In the section from 4:23 to 13:58 he has, so to speak, plowed up the Marcan order and planted five major discourses. With these three areas, accordingly, we shall begin.

In the resurrection story and elsewhere we shall devote our main attention to the Matthean variations from Mark. Of the Marcan material that our author adopts unchanged we can only say (let us say it now once and for all) that it must have served his general design (to give an account of Christ's life) without impeding his special design. He promoted this special design negatively by omitting Marcan matter; he promoted it positively to some extent by transposing Marcan matter; he promoted it most of all by inserting his own "Matthean" matter. It is the content and arrangement of this "Matthean" matter that will chiefly occupy us.

The proper theme of the resurrection story is that of the tomb found empty on Easter morning and of Christ's subsequent apparitions. This, the only theme found in the Marcan, Lucan, and Johannine resurrection stories, we shall call the apparition theme — the "A" theme. Our first gospel, however, has a second theme, purely "Matthean," which tells how the Jewish leaders set guards at the tomb, and what followed their act. We shall call it the guards-at-the-tomb theme, or "G" theme.

The "A" theme of the first gospel is not purely Matthean. It starts with the truncated Marcan resurrection story (Mk 16:1-8), which had told only of the tomb found empty by the women, of the angel's message to them, and of their panic:

> They departed and fled from the tomb, for trembling and fear had seized them; and they said nothing to anyone, for they were afraid.

Discarding some details of this Marcan story, our author changed its ending to open the way for his own matter, the two Matthean apparitions. These two apparitions must play the main role in his "A" theme, as the "A" theme in turn must be the primary theme in his resurrection story; not only is it the proper theme of a resurrection story, it is also the theme with which his story ends.

The "G" theme, too, however, must play an important role. When the author was discarding Marcan details that did not serve his design, he would not hale in a whole new theme, roughly equal in size to the "A" theme, if it did not serve that design in some big way. In some way, of course, that was subordinated to the "A" theme. The action of the secondary theme must contribute somehow to the action of the primary. How was this contribution made? Our first clue is the author's arrangement of the two themes. He cut up each into three pieces: G^1, G^2, G^3; A^1, A^2, A^3. These six pieces he strung like beads alternately on a single thread of narrative: G^1, A^1, G^2, A^2, G^3, A^3— as we can see in the following scheme, with the Matthean elements of the story italicized:

10

"G"   "A"

G¹. *The next day, which was the one after the Day of Prepation, the chief priests and the Pharisees went in a body to Pilate, saying, "Sir, we have remembered how that deceiver said, while he was yet alive, 'After three days I will rise again.' Give orders therefore, that the sepulchre be guarded until the third day, or else his disciples may come and steal him away, and say to the people, 'He has risen from the dead'; and the last imposture will be worse than the first." Pilate said to them, "You have a guard; go, guard it as well as you know how." So they went and made the sepulchre secure, sealing the stone and setting the guard.*

A¹. Now, late in the night of the Sabbath, as the first day of the week began to dawn, Mary Magdalene and the other Mary came to see the sepulchre.

G². *And behold, there was a great earthquake; for an angel of the Lord came down from heaven, and drawing near,* *rolled back the stone and sat on it. His countenance was like lightning, and his raiment like snow. And for fear of him the guards were terrified and became like dead men.*

A². The angel spoke and said to the women, "Do not *you* be *afraid;* for I know that you seek Jesus who was crucified. He is not here, for he has risen as he said. Come, see the place where the Lord was laid. And go quickly, tell his disciples that he has risen; and behold, he goes before you into Galilee; there you shall see him. Behold I have foretold it to you." And they departed *quickly* from the tomb in fear *and great joy, and ran to tell his disciples. And behold, Jesus met them, saying, "Hail!" And they came up and embraced his feet and worshiped him. Then Jesus said to them, "Do not be afraid; go, take word to my brethren that they are to set out for Galilee; there they shall see me." (As) they went* ...

G³. *Some of the guards came into the city and reported to*

the chief priests all that had happened. And when they had assembled with the elders and consulted together, they gave much money to the soldiers, telling them, "Say, 'His disciples came by night and stole him while we were sleeping.' And if the procurator hears of this, we will persuade him and keep you out of trouble." And they took the money, and did as they were instructed; and this story has been spread among the Jews even to this day.

A³. *The eleven disciples went into Galilee to the mountain where Jesus had directed them to go. And when they saw him they worshiped him; but some doubted. And Jesus drew near and spoke to them, saying, "All authority in heaven and on earth has been given to me. Go, therefore, and make disciples of all the nations, baptizing them in the name of the Father and of the Son and of the Holy Spirit, teaching them to observe all that I have commanded you; and behold, I am with you all days, even to the consummation of the world."*

From this scheme we see that the action of the "G" theme can influence that of the "A" theme only at the two points — the inception of A^2 and the inception of A^3— where it penetrates the action of the "A" theme. This being the case, the end action of G^2 should influence the inception of A^2, and the end action of G^3 should influence the inception of A^3.

The end action of G^2 does, in fact, motivate the beginning of the angel's address to the women. Our author has altered the Marcan story to show the motivation. In Mark the angel says to the women, "Do not be amazed, (*mē ekthambeisthe*)." Our author makes him say, "Do not *you* be *afraid*, (*mē phobeisthe hymeis*)," with an obvious reference to the guards prostrated with terror.

Our anticipation that the action of the "G" theme would influence that of the "A" theme at the two points of penetration has thus been verified at the first of those points.

When we come to the second, there are several things to note. First, there is the author's peculiar treatment of the apparition in A^3. This is the climactic event of his book. After the barest of introductions, Jesus speaks to the apostles. The whole interest of the event is centered on his message. The solemnity of the message, the fact that the book stops short as soon as Jesus stops speaking, are hints that we reach in the message the culminating point of the author's design.

What is Christ's message? A command, imposed by the most tremendous authority, to go forth to the Gentile world. The word used in it for "nations" means Gentile nations.

Since both Jesus and the author omit every qualifying phrase or nuance that would allow the apostles to delay before they go forth, to execute unfinished business in Judea, they must go at once. In Luke Jesus gives them their world mission, but tells them to "begin from Jerusalem." That qualifying phrase left them time for the years of their post-ascension mission to the Jewish people, on which we find them engaged in Acts 1 to 12. The postscript to Mark's gospel, too, includes a mandate to the world mission; "Preach the gospel to every *creature*." This form of the mandate, too, left them time for a prior national mission to the Jews; it did not specify "Gentiles," and it did not tell them, "Go."

Now, our author knew about that post-ascension mission of the apostles to the Jewish people, which antedated their world mission. He had alluded to it in 23:34.

If he wanted his reader to see this national mission intervening between Christ's command to go to the Gentiles and the apostles' execution of the command, he had only to insert a qualifying phrase into A^3. By omitting, on the other hand, every qualifying phrase, he would make his readers see the apostles going forth at once, in obedience to that tremendous, unqualified mandate, *with their national mission already behind them.* It is this latter vision that he has evoked; and not only by omitting qualifiers. He has also preceded A^3 by G^3's end action, which both furnishes the motivation for an immediate exodus to the Gentile world, and also puts behind the apostles the years during which they had labored on their national mission.

That end-action told how the Jewish authorities kept spreading a calumny about the apostles "even to this day." What day? The one on which our author, years after the ascension, was penning the conclusion to his book. "Even to this day." That phrase covered all the years of the apostles' national mission. After the Jewish authorities had assiduously poisoned the minds of the Jewish people for so many years, and had frustrated the apostles' mission to them, what was left for them but to go to the Gentiles? "They left Jerusalem."

Thus the author's selection and arrangement of his materials makes a causal nexus appear at the second point where his "G" theme penetrates his "A" theme. And what is the effect he seems to be aiming at by that selection, arrangement, and nexus? To have the apostles leave Jerusalem with their national mission behind them. To make their going a final departure, the final departure that took place many years after the ascension.

He further reinforces this effect by the causal connexion he makes between the first apparition of Christ and the second. In the apparition to the women, as in the later apparition to the Eleven, the whole emphasis is on the command that Jesus gives; the circumstances preceding the command are given briefly, and the account of the apparition stops with the command.

"Go," Jesus commands the apostles, "into Galilee. There you will see me."

It is in obedience to this command that the apostles leave Jerusalem and go to "the mountain to which Jesus had directed them." But why did he summon them from Jerusalem? To give them their commission to go to the Gentiles. Giving them that commission is the only thing he says or does when he meets them; it is, therefore (as our author sees it or wants us to see it), the complete *rason d' etre* for his summons. Such being the case, Jesus must will them to go forth at once. It would be irrational for him to summon them from Jerusalem to assign them to a Gentile mission, if he wanted them first to go back to Jerusalem and spend many years there on a national mission to the Jewish people. Though, as we shall see later, that national mission weighed on the author's mind when he wrote his book, he presents it here as a labor lying not before, but behind the apostles. It is what they leave behind when they leave Jerusalem.

The author has produced this effect with his resurrection story, not while he was engaged on its minor details, when he might supposedly have been distracted by more important considerations. He has produced it by the causal relations he evokes between his two themes, and between his two apparitions, through his manipulation of the contents and arrangement of his story. It is the product of a pervasive molding process; a process that everywhere in the story is at work, choosing this, rejecting that. It looks very much like the product of the author's special design. Indeed, when we consider that the choices that produce it pervade his resurrection story, it looks like his essential design for that story. It is a story with two levels: one of narrative, which pertained to his general design (the composition of a "gospel"); and a higher level of exposition, pertaining to his special design. On this higher level, it seems, he discussed the final departure of the apostles from Jerusalem and explained it as the effect of two causes: one immediate but indirect (the persistent hostility of the Jewish leaders); the other remote but direct (Christ's command, based on his own departure from Jerusalem the day he rose).

Before we proceed to test this hypothesis, let us see what the circumstances of that final departure were.

In Acts 11:29 Luke tells how the Christians of Antioch resolved to send aid to "the brothers dwelling in Judea. This they did, sending it to the elders by the hands of Barnabas and Saul." At that point Luke interrupts his story with a long parenthesis of twenty-four verses and resumes his account of Barnabas and Saul in 12:25. It is the function of a parenthesis to explain something that was just said. The one thing Luke had just said that clamored for explanation was the word "elders." His readers did not have to be told that it meant the ruling body of a Christian community. They were Christians and lived in communities governed by elders. They understood that Barnabas and Saul brought the Antiochene offerings to the rulers of the church of Judea. But elders were not apostles. Luke himself will repeatedly distinguish them from apostles in Acts 15. Therefore the apostles had left Judea. If they were still in Judea, they would be ruling the church there as they had done since Pentecost, and the offerings would have been sent to them. As recently in Luke's story as 11:1-18 they were ruling there; up to that point he had not once mentioned elders. At 11:19 he shifts the scene of action to Antioch, and, when he shifts it back to Jerusalem ten verses later, elders are ruling there. Truly, a change that clamored for explanation. Why had the apostles left? Luke's parenthesis provides the answer.

Herod Agrippa had executed James the brother of John as an experiment, to see how the people took it. They were pleased. So he next seized the leader of the apostles, intending to bring him, too, to summary trial and execution. This second blow at the Christian movement proved equally popular; for Peter, after his miraculous liberation, would congratulate himself on his rescue "from all the expectation of the Jewish people." The popularity of Herod's acts made plain to the other apostles that they faced extermination. They must flee at once, leaving a body of elders to rule the Judean church in their place.

Such was the situation, as Luke's parenthesis portrayed it. Since this situation explained what Luke had to explain, and since his parenthesis does what a parenthesis ought to do, it seems reasonable to conclude that he gives Herod's persecution as the reason why the apostles had left Jerusalem and elders were ruling there.

He names the head of the elders: James. "Tell this to James and the brothers," Peter says before he flees. Who was this James? Again, Luke's readers did not have to be told; as "the brother of the Lord" and leader of Christendom's mother church for twenty years, his name would be familiar to every Christian.[1]

In Acts 15 and 21 the scene of action returns to Jerusalem long enough for us to see who rules there. It is still the elders, headed by James. Theirs had been no caretaker government, lasting only till the persecution ceased and the apostles came back. It was permanent.

In Acts 15 the apostles are in Jerusalem; a fact that has led some to suppose, against the evidence of Acts 11 and 12, that they had never left Judea. They are back; but the elders still rule there. They join the apostles in sending a letter to the Gentile churches, imposing certain observances on them. They assert,

---

1. From early times there have been two traditions about James, the brother of the Lord. The eastern church tended to distinguish him from the apostle James the Less; whereas the western church identified them. Acts 11 and 12 strongly favors the eastern tradition. On the other side there is Paul writing to the Galatians (1:19), "I saw none of the other apostles except James the brother of the Lord." That proof depends, however, on the meaning of the Greek words **ei mē**, which are translated "except." They can also be translated "but" in this sense: "I saw none of the other apostles but (I did see) James the brother of the Lord." For a criticism of other arguments see Wikenhauser, **New Testament Introduction**, New York, 1958, page 480.

equally with the apostles, the divine force of their authority: "It has seemed good to us and the Holy Spirit ... to impose on you only these necessary conditions."

Plainly, these elders rule.

Do they claim jurisdiction over the Gentile churches? We need not suppose so much. The content of the joint letter shows that they sign it as guarantors for the Judean church.

A threat to Christian unity had arisen in that church. The Mosaic Law, which the Jewish Christians observed, forbade Jews to live in community with the uncircumcised. Christians had to live in community with one another, the Church had to be one. On this point all were agreed; so a strong faction of Pharisee converts (the Pharisees were particularly rigorous on maintaining separation from Gentiles) insisted on the circumcision of the Gentile Christians. No solution to the crisis caused by this agitation could be hoped for unless the rulers of the Judean church cooperated and helped to enforce it. When the question had first been raised (in Acts 11), the apostles ruled the Judean church and the apostles settled it. Now that it was raised again, the apostles *together with the elders* met in joint council to settle it; the apostles in virtue of their supreme authority over the whole Church, the elders because they ruled the Church from which the trouble arose.

In the council Peter recalled God's revelation to him; "God through my mouth" had shown that the law must not be imposed on the Gentile converts. The silence that followed his strong words indicated a general acceptance of his doctrine, but also a feeling that it would not ease the qualms of the Jewish Christians. Something more must be said, a compromise must be offered; James, speaking for the Jewish Christians offers one, and it is accepted by all, both apostles and elders. It thus became a compact, ratified by the apostles on behalf of the Gentile churches (on whom they undertook to enforce its terms) and by the elders on behalf of the Judean church. The joint letter to the Gentile churches announced the compact to them.

James and the elders, therefore, rule the Judean church.

Then what are the apostles doing in Jerusalem? Presumably, they are visiting it. Visits by apostles to churches they had founded were not abnormal. Paul (Acts 14:28) visited the churches over which he had appointed elders; he summoned the elders of Ephesus to Miletus (Acts 20:17) when he had no time to visit them.

Peter's opening words to the council seem to imply that he no longer resides in Judea. "In the old days among you," he says, "God decided through my mouth that the Gentiles should hear the word of the gospel and believe."

The "old days" (*hemerōn archaiōn*) could be translated the "first days"; but that would not be true of the event (his baptizing of Cornelius) that Peter refers to, which did not take place in the "first days."

The term "the old days" always contrasts a past state of things with a present one that has replaced it. The past state is always described by a modifier: "the *good* old days"; "the *bad* old days"; "the days of old *when knights were bold.*" The modifier used by Peter is "among you." A state of affairs when someone was among them has passed away. Who was this someone? Apparently God or Peter, since he mentions only these two — and God is still among them. It is Peter, then, who is no longer among them; as a permanent resident, obviously. So he is there, it would seem, only as a visitor. But in that case, Jerusalem has ceased to be the apostles' headquarters; their mission to the Jewish people has ended, and since the other apostles no longer have a reason for residing there, they too should be present merely as visitors.

It is also worth while to ask *how many* apostles were at the council. Paul's account of it names only Peter and John. He writes to the Galatians:

> The men of authority laid no further burden on me. On the contrary, when they saw that to me was committed the gospel for the uncircumcised, as to Peter for the circumcised (for he who worked in Peter for the apostolate of the circumcised worked also in me for the Gentiles)—

and when they recognized the grace that was given to me, James and Cephas and John, who were considered pillars, gave to me and to Barnabas the right hand of fellowship, that we should go to the Gentiles, and they to the circumcised (Gal 2:6-9).

James — whom Paul names first because James' agreement with him was particularly important to Paul's argument — Peter, and John gave him, he asserts, the right hand of fellowship. Did the other apostles refuse to give it? Were they not regarded as pillars? If they gave it, would he fail to say so, when the point at issue was the identity of his doctrine with theirs? The answer to all these questions is a probable no. All things considered, then, it seems likely that he names Peter and John because they alone were present — a conclusion more in harmony with their being visitors than with the hypothesis that the apostles as a body still resided in Jerusalem.

But does not Peter's and John's recognition that the apostolate of the Gentiles had been entrusted to Paul, and the apostolate of the circumcised to themselves, imply that they had not left Palestine and did not intend to do so? Not if that "recognition" is interpreted in the light of the Gentile mission that Peter and John had received from Christ (Mt 28:19; Mk 16:15; Luke 24:47; Acts 1:8). That mandate bound them to evangelize peoples whom their own Galilean background and education had ill equipped them to attack directly, as Paul could. They had to win Jews of the Dispersion first; through these they could reach Gentiles; they could also rule and instruct Gentile churches already founded. Their recognition that Paul's Gentile background and special divine call made him the spearhead of the mission to the Gentiles gives us no grounds, then, for imagining that they did not leave Judea in Herod's persecution to evangelize elsewhere as best they could.

Thus the strong testimony of Acts 11 and 12 is weakened neither by Luke's subsequent words nor by those of Paul. It agrees, moreover, with the ancient tradition that the exodus of the apostles came twelve years after the ascension. The earliest surviving statement of that tradition is in a fragment of a lost work, *The Preaching of Peter*, which goes back to the end of the first or to the beginning of the second century. "The Lord said to the apostles," it reads, "If any of Israel will repent ... his sins shall be forgiven him. After twelve years go out into the inhabited earth."[2] This tradition puts their departure in 42 A.D., during Herod's reign, which lasted from 41 to 44 A.D.

We can take Herod's persecution, therefore, as the probable occasion, and 42 A.D. as a probable date for the exodus of the apostles.

What caused the persecution? Apparently, the policy begun by Peter of admitting Gentiles into the Church without circumcision. Till he baptized Cornelius and set a precedent followed with much success at Antioch, the Jewish populace so venerated the apostles that they had been immune from attack in the persecution that broke out after Stephen's death. The veneration turned to antipathy after the new policy was introduced; Herod found that killing James and arresting Peter pleased the people. The difficulty Jewish Christians had in accepting the new policy gives some idea of the rancor it aroused in the unconverted populace. The crowd in the temple erupted as soon as Paul mentioned his mission to the Gentiles.

> Till he said this they were listening to him, but then they lifted up their voice and shouted, "Away from the earth with such a one! It is not right that he should live." They were shouting and throwing off their garments and casting dust into the air ... (Acts 22:22 ff.).

With one word he had touched the nerve of their bitterness towards the Christian movement.

---

2. The fragment is quoted in Clement of Alexandria, **Stromata VI**, 5, 43.

THE FINAL BREAK

We come now to Christ's temple discourse — a term in which we lump all his words in the temple on Holy Tuesday. The writer of our first gospel bound all those words together into a powerful unity by the great masses of Matthean matter that he concentrated at the beginning (in the three parables) and at the end (in the seven woes and the farewell to Jerusalem). Those Matthean masses and his other changes in the Marcan discourse make the whole discourse lead up to Christ's farewell and to the departure which immediately follows it. They make the farewell represent Christ's final break with Israel. They make his departure a final departure.

They do more than this. They make Christ's final departure represent the final departure of the apostles when they broke off their post-ascension mission to Israel and went to the Gentile world, for the author has Jesus make his final break, farewell, and departure *in view of the Jewish leaders' repulse of that post-ascension mission.* Precisely because they have spurned this final effort of his to save Israel, Jesus finally breaks with Israel. Hence this final break must include the apostles' break-off of that frustrated mission. The departure that executes the final break must include their final departure as well. They go with him; he goes with them.

In the Marcan discourse we find no such ultimates. It has no mention of the apostles' post-ascension mission to the Jewish nation. It has no hint of a final break with the Jewish nation. It has no farewell. The contents of the Marcan discourse are as follows:

1. The Pharisees and the Sadducees challenge Christ's authority; he parries the challenge with a counterquestion.

2. He reviews his mission to Israel in the parable of the vinedressers, and, anticipating his death at the hands of the Jewish leaders, he warns them what their punishment will be.

3. They propose three problems and he solves them.

4. He instructs the people.

5. While resting in the treasury hall, he comments on the generous contribution of the poor widow. Then he leaves.

Our author makes some minor changes in the Marcan material and its arrangements. These changes erase Marcan features that do not fit into the picture of a final clash where the implacable malice of the Jewish leaders is met with an implacable condemnation from Christ. Out goes the idyllic passage about the widow's mites. Out go the friendly comments of the Scribe and of Christ when he solves the third problem. Christ's query about David's son is lifted out of his instruction to the people, and is hurled instead at the Pharisees; this keeps the clash alive. It thus prepares for Christ's warning to the people against the Pharisees; a warning that leads in its turn to the seven woes that Christ pronounces on the Pharisees, and to his farewell.

Thus these minor changes help to unify the Matthean discourse, so that it flows unbroken from the opening challenge to the final farewell.

It is the big masses of Matthean material, however, that must carry the main burden of the author's design. The two biggest, as we have said, occur at the beginning and at the end of the discourse. A third, smaller mass before the end, takes the shape of an exhortation: a farewell instruction to Christ's followers. This instruction we shall look at later. We begin our study of the discourse with Christ's seven woes and the farewell that follows them.

His seven maledictions are aimed directly at the Pharisees, the most influential of the Jewish sects and the one most responsible for the people's rejection of him. Since, however, it is their *ruinous* leadership of the people that he inveighs against, the people themselves come within the scope of the doom that he pronounces.

His first woe is a general denunciation of their leadership and its disastrous effect: the exclusion of the people from the messianic kingdom.

> Woe to you Scribes and Pharisees, hypocrites! because you shut the kingdom of heaven against men. You yourselves do not go in, nor do you permit those going in to enter.

The next five woes fasten on various aspects of their evil influence.

> Woe to you Scribes and Pharisees, hypocrites! because you traverse sea and land to make one convert. When he has become one, you make him twofold more a son of hell than yourselves.
>
> Woe to you, blind guides, who say, "Whoever swears by the temple, it is nothing; but whoever swears by the gold of the temple, he is bound." You blind fools! which is greater, the gold or the temple that sanctifies the gold? And, "Whoever swears by the altar, it is nothing; but whoever swears by the gift that is on it, he is bound." Blind ones! which is greater, the gift or the altar that sanctifies the gift? Therefore he who swears by the altar swears by it and by all things that are on it; and he who swears by heaven swears by the throne of God and by him who sits on it.
>
> Woe to you Scribes and Pharisees, hypocrites! because you pay tithes on mint and anise and cummin, and have left undone the weightiest matters of the Law, justice and mercy and faith. These things you ought to have done while not leaving the others undone. Blind guides, who strain out the gnat and swallow the camel!

> Woe to you Scribes and Pharisees, hypocrites! because you clean the outside of the cup and the dish, but within they are full of robbery and uncleanness. Thou blind Pharisee! clean first the inside of the cup and of the dish, that the outside may be clean.
>
> Woe to you Scribes and Pharisees, hypocrites! because you are like whited sepulchres, which outwardly appear to men beautiful, but within are full of dead men's bones and of all uncleanness. So you also outwardly appear just to men, but within are full of hypocrisy and iniquity.

The seventh woe describes their crowning transgression; theirs and that of the whole line of Jewish leaders before them since the nation began. The history of Israel as God's people reaches its culmination here. Its measure is filled up.

> Woe to you Scribes and Pharisees, hypocrites! you build the sepulchres of the prophets and adorn the tombs of the just and say, "If we had lived in the days of our fathers, we would not have been their accomplices in the blood of the prophets." Thus you are witnesses against yourselves that you are the sons of those who killed the prophets. You too — fill up the measure of your fathers!

Jesus himself furnishes them the occasion for filling the measure up by assigning his apostles to their post-ascension mission to Israel. It is the apostles whom he calls "prophets"; as he had already done in other Matthean passages of the gospel (5:12; 10:41). Other Christian leaders are referred to as "wise men" and "scribes."

> Serpents, brood of vipers, how are you to escape the judgment of hell? For this reason, see, I am sending you prophets and wise men and scribes. Some of them you will put to death and crucify, and some you will scourge

in your synagogues and persecute from town to town; that upon you may come all the just blood that has been shed on the earth from the blood of Abel the just to the blood of Zacharias the son of Barachias, whom you killed between the temple and the altar. Amen I say to you, all these things will come on this generation.

On this generation. The Jewish people, because they have accepted the evil leadership of the Scribes and Pharisees, are enveloped in this immense disaster. Having reviewed their repulse of his final effort to save them, Jesus says good-bye to the Jewish nation:

Jerusalem, Jerusalem, thou that killest the prophets and stonest those who are sent to thee! How often would I have gathered thy children together, as a hen gathers her young ones under her wings, but thou wouldst not! Behold, your house is left to you empty. For I say to you, you shall not see me from now on till you say, "Blessed is he who comes in the name of the Lord!"

Thus the Savior of Israel abandons the nation. The abandonment is total and final. He will make no further efforts to save them. He leaves their house (the temple) to them — empty. They will not see him again till his return at the end of the world. And this abandonment starts *now*: "You shall not see me *from now on.*"

He executes his sentence at once: "He left the temple and went away."

Let us stop here to consider the author's intention in inserting the seventh woe, and the good-bye to Jerusalem, and in tying them together as he has done. Why did he intrude an unmistakable description of the apostles' post-ascension mission in Jerusalem? Why did he stress that it was God's final effort to save the Jewish nation? The effort whose bloody repulse filled up the measure of Israel's guilt, and entailed the nation's destruction? Why did he follow that description of the final effort with a final good-bye; and why did he make the repulse of all Christ's efforts the motive for that last farewell? How could he tie those two passages together without intending to assert a causal nexus between them? And how could he assert this causal nexus without intending to make Christ's denunciation of a final break represent the apostles' break-off of their national mission when they left Jerusalem to go to the Gentiles? How could he do all this without intending to make the departure of Jesus, which symbolizes the final break, symbolize the final departure of the apostles? Through all his insertions and rearrangements he is looking at that final departure.

He had already, as a matter of fact, produced these identical effects, with the same appearance of design, in the climactic third parable at the beginning of the temple discourse.

The three parables review the three phases of Christ's salvific mission to Israel, and the repulse of each by the Jewish leaders. The first phase was John the Baptist's preaching. This phase is reviewed in the parable of the two sons (21:28-32). Although this parable is Matthean, it seems to perform only the minor function of giving explicit consideration to, and an explicit judgment on, this preparatory phase of the mission.

The second phase was that of Jesus' own personal ministry. This is reviewed in the parable of the vinedressers. The parable is Marcan; but it has a Matthean postscript of great importance, which we shall consider in a moment.

The final phase was the post-ascension mission of the apostles in Jerusalem. It is reviewed in the purely Matthean parable of the Marriage Feast.

> The kingdom of heaven is like a king who made a marriage feast for his son. He sent servants to call those invited to the marriage feast, but they would not come. . . .

Who are these servants? Perhaps the Old Testament prophets. Their prophecies, fulfilled in Jesus, announce to the Jewish leaders (cf. Lk 16:29-31; Jn 5:39-46) that the messianic kingdom has arrived.

About the identity of the second party of servants sent by the king there can be no mistake:

> Again he sent out servants, saying, "Tell those who are invited, 'Behold, I have prepared my dinner; my oxen and fatlings are killed, and everything is ready; come to the marriage feast.'" But they made light of it and went off, one to his farm and another to his business; and the rest laid hold of his servants, treated them shamefully, and killed them. When the king heard of it, he was angry; and he sent his armies, destroyed those murderers, and burnt their city. Then he said to his servants, "The marriage feast is ready, but those who were invited were unworthy. Go, therefore, to the crossroads and invite whomever you will find. . . ."

This second party of servants who come to the Jewish people ("those who are invited") with a final call after the messianic feast has been fully prepared, and whose repulse, culminating in a murderous attack, fills up the measure of Israel's guilt, can only be the apostles on their post-ascension mission. We note, moreover, how the King's command to them to go to the Gentiles, because "those who were invited were unworthy," resembles Christ's command at the end of the gospel: "Go, therefore, to the crossroads and invite whomever you find," is a close paraphrase of, "Going, therefore, make disciples of all the nations."

The remainder of the parable completes that parallel; it makes explicit what is implied in Christ's promise, "I will be with you all days even to the consummation of the world":

> His servants went out into the roads and gathered all whom they found, both good and bad; and the marriage feast was filled with guests.
>
> Now the king went in to see the guests, and he saw there a man who had not on a wedding garment. He said to him, "Friend, how didst thou come in here without

a wedding garment?" He was speechless. Then the king said to the attendants, "Bind his hands and feet and cast him forth into the darkness outside, where there will be the weeping and gnashing of teeth." For many are called but few are chosen.

The place of that last paragraph in the author's design will become clear later on in this study. Omitting it for the present, we merely point out that he did not intend to present the apostles' departure to the Gentiles as posterior to the destruction of Jerusalem. He knew — and Jesus knew — that their world mission preceded the capital's destruction: "This gospel of the kingdom will be preached in the whole world for a witness to all nations, *and then will come the end*" (24:14). The order in which the two events are presented is not chronological, therefore, but that of the narrator's convenience. Having two effects of the same act to recount, he disposes first of the one that is not his main topic, in order to clear the way for the other, which is the fact that chiefly interests him — the fact he wants to dwell on. Thus, the fact that chiefly interests our author in his climactic parable, the event he principally looked at in his organization of the three parables, was the apostles' break-off of their mission in Jerusalem and their departure to the Gentile world. That event is explicit, it is final, it is the point at which he rests. And it is, as we have already seen, the event that is symbolized in the farewell and departure of Jesus, which is the climax and goal of the entire, unified, Matthean temple discourse.

We conclude, then, that the author's design in the temple discourse was to discuss the apostles' final departure from Jerusalem, and to assign as its immediate cause the hostility of the Jewish authorities, which had frustrated their mission in Jerusalem.

But this immediate cause was not the only one that he wished to stress. There was another, radical cause: Christ's own abandonment of Israel in favor of the Gentiles. To stress this was the object of his postscript to the Marcan parable of the vinedressers. In the Marcan parable God's punishment for the killing of the Messias falls only on the Jewish leaders. They are to be destroyed and replaced by others:

> "He will utterly destroy those evil men, and will let out the vineyard to other vinedressers, who will render to him the fruits in their seasons."
>
> Jesus said to them, "Did you never read in the Scriptures, 'The stone that the builders rejected has become the cornerstone; by the Lord this has been done, and it is wonderful in our eyes'?"

At this point our author inserts his postscript and widens the scope of God's punishment to include Israel itself. It is to be replaced by another people — by a Gentile people, therefore. It has forfeited its messianic destiny, and if it continues to harass Christ's work (this part of the postscript opens the way for the third parable), it will be destroyed:

> Therefore I say to you that the kingdom of God will be taken from you and will be given to a people yielding its fruits. And he who falls on this stone will be broken to pieces; and him on whom it falls it will grind to powder (21:43 ff.).

Let us see how this postscript completes the Matthean design for the temple discourse. The transfer of the kingdom from the Jewish nation to the Gentiles is the punishment decreed for the death of Christ. It will take place, consequently, three days later at the moment when he dies. At that moment God's favor is definitively withdrawn from Israel. It is a final juridical break. And as such it determines in advance the nature and course of the apostles' post-ascension mission in Jerusalem. It can only be temporary; their permanent mission is to the Gentiles. And it is foredoomed to frustration by the Jewish leaders' hostility; foredoomed to be broken off when that hostility reaches the

point of killing the apostles. Thus the departure of the apostles
from Jerusalem was decreed years before by Christ's final break
with Israel on Good Friday.

Now this break is the thing that Christ announces at the end
of the temple discourse in his farewell to Jerusalem. He makes
it take the shape of his own final departure from Jerusalem.
"You shall not see me from now on." Thus our author's innovations
term the exit of Jesus from the temple and city on Holy Tuesday
into a symbol both of God's juridical break with Israel on Good
Friday, and of the kingdom's de-facto transfer years later. Both
those events are seen as a *departure from Jerusalem.* The symbol
of the juridical break is Christ's personal departure; the symbol
of the de-facto transfer is the apostles' departure.

The author has laid down in his temple discourse the blueprint of a resurrection story. This resurrection story will contain
two departures from Jerusalem; that of Jesus as soon as he rises
on Easter, and that of the apostles. The second departure will
have two causes; a direct and an indirect, a remote and an immediate. Remotely but directly, it will be demanded by Jesus' own
departure. Immediately but indirectly, it will be compelled by
the malice of Jewish leaders. And its goal will be to launch
the world mission to which the apostles are appointed.

Those, neither more nor less, are the contents of the resurrection story required by the Matthean temple discourse. Those,
neither more nor less, are the contents of the Matthean resurrection story. This exact correspondence cannot be due to chance.
The author intended this discourse to be a blueprint for his
story.

Let us recall the hypothesis we formed in the first chapter
about the Matthean resurrection story. From its structure and
contents we concluded that the writer intended to present the
apostles' departure as their final departure from Jerusalem, and
to explain it as due to two causes; an immediate indirect cause
(Jewish malice), and a remote direct one (Christ's command,
rooted in his own departure from Jerusalem on Easter Sunday).

That hypothesis has been confirmed.

We look now at Christ's farewell instruction to the crowds and his disciples:

The Scribes and Pharisees sit on the chair of Moses. All things, therefore, that they command you, observe and do. But do not act according to their works; for they talk but do nothing. They bind together heavy and oppressive burdens and lay them on men's shoulders, but not with one finger do they wish to move them. In fact, they do all their works in order to be seen by men. They widen their phylacteries and enlarge their tassels and love the first places at suppers and the front seats in the synagogues, and greetings in the market-place, and to be called Rabbi. But do not you be called Rabbi; for one is your teacher and all you are brothers. And call no one on earth your father; for one is your father, who is in heaven. Nor be called masters; for one alone is your Master: the Christ. He who is greatest among you shall be called your servant. And whoever exalts himself shall be humbled, and whoever humbles himself shall be exalted (23:1-12).

Since Christ's departure at the end of the temple discourse represents the apostles' own departure at the end of their mission in Jerusalem, should not Christ's farewell before the departure, and the discourse leading up to that farewell, represent the apostles' own farewell to the Jewish nation?

Should not Christ's review of his efforts to save Israel — a review intended to justify his break with the nation — be the apostles's own justification for going to the Gentiles?

Should not that parting instruction of Christ to the followers he was leaving behind under a Jewish government dominated by the Pharisees be the apostles' own parting instruction to the Judean church?

This is the new hypothesis that we must test. It supposes that the gospel as a whole, and not merely the temple discourse, was addressed to the Judean church. It supposes, moreover, that the apostles would represent a message from themselves to be a message from Christ. Both those suppositions must be verified. The rest of the gospel must furnish evidence that it was addressed to the Judean church. The rest of the gospel must stress that the authority of the apostles was equivalently Christ's; so that when they spoke, he spoke. And both these kinds of evidence must be *Matthean;* not found in Mark, but due to our author's innovations.

3

THE PLOWED-UP AREA: I. AN EXHORTATION

The plowed-up area (Mt 4:23-13:58, corresponding to Mk 1:21-6:13) has some unique features. Outside it our author changes the Marcan order of events only once, when he puts the cleansing of the temple before the cursing of the fig tree; but inside it he radically rearranges that order. Into it, moreover, he packs an exceptional amount of his own material, especially in the five discourses. One of these is purely Matthean; another, the sermon on the mount, is Matthean except for a few Marcan scraps; the others are built on Marcan originals, much altered and expanded.

While those features suggest the writer's intense preoccupation with his special design, two others hint at a unified function for the area. One is the continuity imposed throughout the area by various linking devices; the other is the area-wide sweep of his rearrangements. He moves the Marcan choice of the Twelve from the middle of the area to the front, and the Marcan mission of the twelve from the rear to the middle; the Marcan miracles, which had stood in two groups at the front and the back of the area, he masses immediately after the sermon on the mount. To discover what plan underlies all this activity, we must study the three sections of the area separately; a task that will engage us in this and the next two chapters.

He devotes the first section (4:23-7:29) to the sermon on the mount. This he presents as a unified discourse by recalling at the end the circumstances in which it began. He began it with "Seeing *the crowds,* Jesus went up *the mountain.* And when he was seated, his disciples came to him. And opening his mouth, he *taught* them." He ends it with "When Jesus had finished these words, *the crowds* were astonished at his *teaching.* .... And when he came down from *the mountain.* ..." Here again are the mountain, the crowds, and Jesus teaching them — the same place, listeners, and action. There is no mention of the disciples at the end; the sermon was aimed principally, it would seem, at the crowds.

The narrative that introduces it is the Marcan introduction (Mk 3:7-13) to Christ's choice of the Twelve. That event, of capital importance, our author drops. He wishes us to see the Twelve in "the disciples" who come to Jesus on the mountain; he keeps referring to them afterwards by the same term till he reaches 10:1, where he gives their number: they are "the twelve disciples" and in the next verse "the twelve apostles." Though he omits Christ's *choice* of them, he nevertheless provides a substitute. On that Galilean mountain Christ *appoints them to their world mission.*

Before the body of the sermon stand the eight beatitudes (addressed primarily, like the body of the sermon, to the crowds), and this passage addressed exclusively to the Twelve:

> Blessed are you when men insult you and persecute you, and speaking falsely, say all manner of evil against you, for my sake. Rejoice and exult, because your reward is great in heaven; for so did they persecute the prophets before you.

The persecution evoked in those lines is the one described in the seventh woe of the temple discourse: there, as here, the apostles are the successors of the prophets, and their enemies are those who persecuted the prophets. The persecution, be it noted, can be a present one; for the author has omitted the phrase, "in that day," which Luke includes (Lk 6:23) when recording this passage, and which would make the persecution a future one.

After saluting the Twelve thus, Christ gives them their world mission: "You are the salt of the earth. . . . You are the light of the world." It is a task they are to act on at once:

> A city set on a mountain cannot be hid. Neither do men light a lamp and put it under a bushel, but on the lamp-stand, so as to give light to all in the house. Even so let your light shine before men.

Here, then, at the beginning of Christ's discourse the author has placed the scene and the act with which his gospel ends: the mountain in Galilee, and the world mission given to the apostles who come to Christ approved by their endurance of persecution at Jewish hands.

Who are the crowds to whom the beatitudes are addressed? The eighth is linked by its theme and opening words with the salute to the apostles: "Blessed are they who suffer persecution for justice sake. . . . Blessed are you when men insult and persecute you . . . for my sake."

When Christ turns from the beatitude to the salute, from the crowds to the Twelve, he sees the same blessedness in persecution. The same blessedness. Is not the persecution, then, the same? Are not these crowds those who were to share with the apostles the persecution predicted in the seventh woe: "Behold, I am sending you prophets *and wise men and scribes*"? Are these crowds the Judean church?

The body of the sermon deals with the "justice" required for the messianic kingdom. Two facts stand out in it. First, it was addressed to the Judean church. It starts abruptly with a warning against the "justice" of the Scribes and Pharisees; then for more than half its length it lists Pharisaic doctrines and practices that must be avoided. The doctrines would be known only to Jews; the practices, for the most part, would not be found outside of Palestine. In what Gentile city, for instance, would one find hypocrites praying at the street corners?

Our author, let us remember, did not put material into his gospel simply because he knew it. He knew much — even of great importance, like the choice of the Twelve — that he omitted because it did not serve his purpose. He inserted things because they served his purpose. What purpose could he serve by warning Gentile Christians against doctrines "you have heard," that they had not heard; or against practices they had not seen and would consider outlandish? What good was done by warning them not to use the word *Raca,* a word he does not explain, and that has never been explained, but was apparently a piece of offensive Palestinian slang?

The instruction makes sense, then, only as addressed to Palestinian Jews. This is the first fact that stands out in it. The second is that it exactly corresponds to the instruction in the temple discourse.

That instruction, too, will be addressed to "the crowds and his disciples." It, too, will start with an abrupt warning against the Scribes and Pharisees. It will have these five themes: 1. It will warn against the ostentatious practices of the Scribes and Pharisees. 2. It will proscribe their teaching: "for one, only one is your Teacher: the Christ." 3. It will propose a filial devotion towards God because he is "your Father, who is in heaven." 4. It will command unselfish charity towards other men because "you are all brothers." 5. It will command humility; "he who exalts himself shall be humbled, and he who humbles himself shall be exalted."

Those five themes sum up the instruction in the sermon on the mount. They are the stuff from which it is woven.

To conclude. The first of Christ's discourses is given at a place and time that seem to anticipate those at the end of the gospel. Its instruction corresponds to the one in the temple discourse; it expatiates on the themes that will be there summed up. It is addressed to the Judean church. It is preceded by a passage stressing the authority of the apostles as prophets, and illuminators of the world.

Such are the effects of the author's innovations in this first section of the plowed-up area.

4

THE PLOWED-UP AREA:
II. THE SPURNED CREDENTIALS

Chapters 8, 9, 10, and 11 form a structural unit, the middle section of the plowed-up area. A series of miracles fills 8 and most of 9. The rest of 9 describes Christ's evangelizing of the "lost sheep of Israel" and his commissioning of the Twelve to carry the good news to the exploited masses he cannot personally reach. His instructions to the Twelve fill chapter 10. In chapter 11 he points to his miracles and his evangelization of the masses as proofs that he is the Messias.

"Art thou he who is to come?" John's disciples ask him.

"Tell John what you have seen and heard," he replies. Miracles: "the blind see, the lame walk, the lepers are cleansed, the deaf hear, the dead rise." And the abandoned masses evangelized: "the poor have the good news brought to them."

The discourse of chapter 11 (the one purely Matthean discourse in the gospel), assays the worth of those proofs, and the worthlessness of the Jewish leaders' pretexts for rejecting them. This rejection is the main topic of the discourse: "blessed is he who is not scandalized in me."

Thus the whole section, all four chapters of it, constitutes an indictment of the leaders, and of the people swayed by them. This indictment corresponds exactly, as we shall see, to the first part of the Matthean temple discourse — the three parables in which Christ will review his mission to Israel and Israel's rejection of him.

The writer ties his train of miracles to the sermon on the mount, and thus links the second section of the plowed-up area with the first. He introduces the first miracle (a leper's cure) with the clause, "When he came down from the mountain"; thus making the miracle continuous with the sermon in place and time. He further establishes a continuity of theme by presenting the sermon and the miracles as complementary aspects of Christ's authority as Son of God. In the sermon that authority took a juridical form; Christ asserted his absolute dominion over creatures. The form it takes in the miracles is physical; Christ performs them by mere expressions of his will. Between the sermon and the miracles stands a transferred Marcan verse:

> When Jesus had finished these words, the crowds were astonished at his teaching; for he taught them as one having authority.

"Authority" in that sentence squints; it looks back to the juridical authority asserted in the sermon, and forward to the physical "authority" displayed in the miracles. The centurion in the second anecdote (a Matthean one) expresses this new concept of authority:

> Only say the word and my servant shall be healed. For I too am a man under authority and have soldiers under me; and I say to one, "Go," and he goes; and to another, "Come," and he comes; and to my servant, "Do this," and he does it.

While the anecdote is thus unifying the whole chain of miracles by its concept of authority, it also forecasts the transfer of the kingdom to the Gentiles:

> Many will come from the east and the west and will feast with Abraham and Isaac and Jacob in the kingdom of heaven, but the children of the kingdom will be cast forth into the darkness outside (8:11 ff.).

A second Matthean insertion (8:17) notes a messianic prophecy fulfilled by the miracles. A third (8:18-22) gives Christ's answers to two prospective followers. The answers have no connection with the review of his credentials; they announce the theme of readiness for total sacrifice which he will expound in chapter 10.

Two incidents of petty criticism (9:9-17) interrupt the series of miracles; they illustrate the Jewish leaders' pretexts for rejecting Christ, and he will speak of them in chapter 11. Then come four more miracles, of which the last two are Matthean. The writer had to insert one (the cure of two blind men) because cures of this sort were the first on Jesus' list —"the blind see"— and there was no Marcan cure of blindness in the plowed-up area. The other Matthean miracle (the cure of a demoniac, 9:32-34) serves the author as a transition to Christ's evangelization of the "poor."

When Jesus said to John's disciples, "The poor have the good news preached to them," he implied that the event fulfilled messianic prophecies. The "poor" in those prophecies (for example, in Isaias 11:3; 29:18 ff.; and 41:17) signified the Jewish masses, exploited, betrayed, and abandoned by their leaders; in one of the most memorable (Ezechiel 34) the prophet called the people lost sheep, and their leaders "the shepherds of Israel." This image of the people as "the lost sheep of the house of Israel" appears in the first gospel as soon as the Pharisees begin to pervert the crowds:

> There was brought to him a dumb man, possessed by a devil. And when the devil had been cast out, the dumb man spoke. The crowds marveled, saying, "Never has the like been seen in Israel." But the Pharisees said, "By the prince of devils he casts out devils."

This picture of Jesus follows at once:

> Jesus was going about all the towns and villages, teaching in their synagogues and preaching the good news of the kingdom and curing every kind of disease and in-

firmity. But seeing the crowds, he was moved with compassion for them, because they were bewildered and dejected, like sheep without a shepherd (9:35 ff.).

In those lines the writer sums up the credentials of unwearied evangelization and of profuse miracles that were presented by Jesus in his personal ministry.

The mission of the Twelve, superimposed by our author on the Marcan, is their *post-ascension mission to Israel*.

The Marcan mission is, in the first place, a much smaller business.

> He summoned the Twelve and began to send them forth two by two; and he gave them power over the unclean spirits. . . . And he said to them, "Wherever you enter into a house, stay there till you leave the place. And whoever does not receive you or heed you — go forth from there, and shake off the dust of your feet for a witness against them." Going forth, they preached that men should repent, and they cast out many devils, anointed with oil many sick people and healed them (Mk 6:6-13).

The miraculous powers of the Twelve on that mission are less ample than Christ's; their authority is modest; and their message is not the joyous Good News — they preach penance.

The Matthean mission, on the other hand, is in the fullest sense the prolongation, expansion, and completion of Christ's own.

> He said to his disciples, "The harvest is great, but the laborers are few. Pray therefore the Lord of the harvest to send forth laborers into his harvest." Then, summoning his twelve disciples, he gave them power over unclean spirits, and to cast them out and to cure every kind of disease and infirmity. . . . These twelve Jesus sent forth,

having instructed them thus: "Do not go in the direction of the Gentiles ... but go rather to the lost sheep of the house of Israel. And as you go, preach, saying 'The kingdom of heaven is at hand!' Cure the sick, raise the dead, cleanse the lepers, cast out devils. Freely you have received, freely give.... And whoever does not receive you, or listen to your words — go forth outside that house or town, and shake off the dust from your feet. Amen I say to you, it will be more tolerable for Sodom and Gomorrha in the day of judgment than for that town" (9:37-10:15).

The miraculous powers of the Twelve on this mission match Christ's own: to cure "every kind of disease and infirmity." They are ordered to use those powers without stint: "raise the dead, cleanse the lepers ... freely you have received, freely give." Their authority is tremendous; woe to the city that refuses to heed them! And they bring the Good News to the "poor"— to the lost sheep of the house of Israel.

These contrasts between the Marcan and the Matthean mission are suggestive, but the crucial difference is in the reception they encounter. The Marcan mission meets no opposition. The Matthean runs into bloody persecution.

> Behold, I am sending you like sheep in the midst of wolves. Be wise therefore as serpents and simple as doves (10:16).

After this ominous prelude the writer casts off all disguise. Borrowing a passage from the Marcan eschatological discourse (Mk 13:9-13), he presents the post-ascension mission of the Twelve to Israel.

> Beware of men; they will deliver you up to councils and scourge you in their synagogues, and you will be brought before governors and kings for my name's sake, for a witness to them and to the Gentiles.... Brother will

hand over his brother to death, and the father his child; children will rise up against parents and put them to death. And you will be hated by all men for my name's sake; but he who perseveres to the end will be saved.

That unmistakably is the persecution the apostles suffered, together with the Judean church, in their post-ascension mission at Jerusalem.

Christ next states the circumstances in which the mission is to be abandoned:

When they persecute you in this city flee to that. Amen I say to you, you will not finish the cities of Israel till the Son of Man comes.

They are to leave because Israel, rejecting Christ and rejected by him, will not be saved till his return at the end of the world. Their departure will be a flight.

The writer's purpose is plain. He has presented the apostles' post-ascension mission to the Jewish people, its reception, and its abandonment, in the same colors as on Holy Tuesday. Here, as there, he makes it the sequel and the climax of Christ's personal mission. And this he does in order that Christ, answering John's disciples, may point to the credentials, of miracles and evangelization, given in that post-ascension mission of the apostles, just as he points to those given in his own personal ministry.

The second part of Christ's instructions in chapter 10 is addressed to all who share with the apostles the Jewish persecution. That is to say, it is addressed to the Judean church. It demands of them, and of all Christ's followers, a readiness for total sacrifice in giving witness to him.

This is the writer's second instruction to the Judean church; his first was the one in the sermon on the mount. Like that earlier one, it is accompanied by a stress on the apostles' authority. In fact, by a double stress. Christ at the beginning of the instruction threatened dire punishment to those who would not heed them. At the end he promises a prophet's reward to those who do heed them, for they are Christ's prophets, who speak in his name. When they speak, he speaks:

> He who receives you, receives me; and he who receives me, receives him who sent me. He who receives a prophet as a prophet shall receive a prophet's reward.

The likeness of the second section of the plowed-up area to the parables of the temple discourse is now perceptible. Those three parables will review the three phases of Christ's mission to Israel: his herald's ministry, his own, and his apostles' after him. When he replies to John's disciples in chapter 11, he points to the proofs he gave of his messianic kingship in the second and the third of those phases. As soon as the emissaries from John leave, he completes the pattern by pointing to John's own credentials: a character so towering that all the people took John for a prophet, and some for the Messias himself:

> What did you go out into the desert to see? ... What did you go out to see? A prophet? Yes, I tell you, and more than a prophet. This is he of whom it is written, "Behold, I send my messenger before thy face, who shall make ready thy way before thee.". . . And if you are willing to receive it, he is Elias who is to come (7-15).

Such was the grandeur of his herald. Yet that grandeur paled before the magnificence of membership in the kingdom to which Jesus invited Israel.

> Among those born of women there has not risen a greater than John the Baptist. Yet the least in the kingdom of heaven is greater than he.

But what has been Israel's response to the invitation?

> From the days of John the Baptist until now the
> kingdom of heaven has endured violence, and the violent
> snatch it away.

To spurn such an invitation, to reject proofs so ample as his,
on pretexts as trivial as those of the Pharisees, was childish folly.
That folly has spread from them to the Jewish people as a whole
—"this generation."

> To what shall I liken this generation? It is like children
> sitting in the market place, who call to their companions
> and say, "We have piped to you and you have not danced;
> we have sung dirges and you have not mourned." For
> John came neither eating nor drinking, and they say, "He
> has a devil!" The Son of Man came eating and drinking,
> and they say, "Behold a glutton and a wine-drinker, a
> friend of publicans and sinners!" And wisdom is justified
> by her works (16-19).

Christ's review of his credentials ends there. Its relation to
his review of his mission on Holy Tuesday is obvious. It supplies
the essential element that will be missing then in his judgment
of the Jewish leaders. He will indict them for rejecting him
though they knew in some degree that he was the Son of God.
"This is the heir," he will make them say. Where did he prove
that charge? Here in the second section of the plowed-up area,
with miracles that revealed him as incarnate God, and with
other signs of his authority.

Two passages annexed to the discourse put the final touch to
the resemblance between this part of the plowed-up area and
the parables of the temple discourse. Christ's review of his
mission ends halfway through the parable of the marriage feast.
The rest of that parable consists of two passages describing
Jerusalem's destruction and the transfer of the kingdom to the
Gentiles. To those two correspond the annexed passages of the
discourse in chapter 11.

The first foretells the destruction of the Galilean towns:

> Woe to thee, Corozain! woe to thee, Bethsaida! . . . And thou, Capharnaum, shalt thou be exalted to heaven? Thou shalt be thrust down into hell. For if the miracles had been worked in Sodom that have been worked in thee, it would have remained to this day. But I tell you, it will be more tolerable for the land of Sodom in the day of judgment than for thee (11:20-24).

The second passage introduces the two parties who will be involved in the transfer of the kingdom. They are the faithful servants whom the King will despatch to the crossroads of the world, and the Gentile masses to whom they will bring his invitation. Here are the faithful servants:

> I praise thee, Father, lord of heaven and earth, that thou didst hide these things from the wise and prudent, and didst reveal them to little ones.

And here are the masses of humanity whom Christ invites:

> Come to me, all you that labor and are burdened . . . take my yoke on you and learn of me . . . and you will find rest for your souls.

Why does the writer, annexing those two passages to the discourse, make them stand half outside it? Why does he furnish each with its own introduction? Because they announce themes that he will develop in the two big discourses of the final section of the plowed-up area. Serving as a transition to that section, they establish its continuity with this second one.

5

THE PLOWED-UP AREA:
III. THE TRANSFER OF THE KINGDOM

The two incidents that begin the third section have each a Matthean insertion. Replying to the Pharisaic accusation against his disciples (an indirect attack on himself), Christ says:

> I tell you that one greater than the temple is here. And if you knew what "I want mercy and not sacrifice" means, you would never have condemned the innocent (12:6-8).

The relation between Christ and the temple is, of course, that of the owner to his house; how this fits into the Matthean scheme will appear later. The rest of the insertion supports the charge Christ will make in the fourth woe of Holy Tuesday: "You pay tithes on mint and anise and cummin, but you have left undone the great things of the Law — justice and mercy and faith." Here the Pharisees display their injustice and mercilessness. They have shown their lack of faith from the start.

When, in the second incident, they plot to kill Christ, our author inserts an Isaian prophecy. It lauds Christ's patience but also, looking forward, it forecasts his victorious judgment on his enemies and the salvation of the Gentiles — the themes of the two big discourses of this section.

> Behold my servant whom I have chosen, my beloved, in whom my soul delights. I will put my Spirit on him, and he will declare judgment to the Gentiles. He will

not wrangle nor cry aloud, nor will anyone hear his voice in the streets. A bruised reed he will not break, a smoking wick he will not quench, till he send forth judgment unto victory; and in his name will the Gentiles hope (12:17-20).

The forecast of victorious judgment is elaborated in the usurped-house discourse.

In Mark the discourse is as follows:

They came to the house, and again a crowd gathered so that they could not so much as take their food. When his own people had heard of it, they went out to lay hold of him, for they said, "He has gone mad." And the Scribes who had come down from Jerusalem said, "He has Beelzebub," and "By the prince of devils he casts out devils." He called them together and said to them in parables:

"How can Satan cast out Satan? And if a kingdom is divided against itself, that kingdom cannot stand. And if a house is divided against itself, that house cannot stand. And if Satan has risen up against himself, he is divided and cannot stand, but is at an end. But no one can enter the strong man's house and plunder his goods, unless he first binds the strong man. Then he will plunder his house.

"Amen I say to you that all sins shall be forgiven to the sons of men, and the blasphemies wherewith they may blaspheme; but whoever blasphemes against the Holy Spirit never has forgiveness, but will be guilty of an everlasting sin."

For they said, "He has an unclean spirit" (Mk 3:20-30).

Taking that original our author made these changes. He replaced the prelude with the cure of the demoniac that had already served him in 9:32-34; he inserted two passages; he added a whole new part; and he bound both parts into unity by recalling in the peroration the situation he had set forth in the prelude. When he finished, his discourse bore a striking resemblance to the woes-and-farewell of the temple discourse.

Here is his prelude.

> There was brought to him a possessed man who was blind and dumb; and he cured him so that he spoke and saw. All the crowds were amazed and they said, "Can this be the Son of David?" But the Pharisees hearing this said, "He does not cast out devils except by Beelzebub, the prince of devils" (12:22-24).

Why did he use that incident again? First, for its symbolism; the image of a possessed man will return in the peroration of the discourse. Second, because both the wavering of the crowds and the poisoned suggestions of their leaders and to be condemned by Christ in the Matthean insertions of the first part of the discourse. Leaders and masses, lumped together in their diverse measures of guilt ("this generation" of his seventh Holy Tuesday woe), will become the "wicked and adulterous generation" whose doom is announced in the second part of the discourse.

The first insertion is aimed at the crowds. Christ unmasks their leaders' insincerity by a simple argument *ad hominem*:

> If I cast out devils by Beelzebub, by whom do your disciples cast them out? Therefore they shall be your judges. But if I cast out devils by the Spirit of God, then the kingdom of God has come on you.

Then he warns the waverers. They are involving themselves in the punishment reserved for his enemies:

> He who is not with me is against me, and he who does not gather with me scatters (11:27-30).

In the second insertion he turns on the leaders with words

that will be echoed in the seventh woe: "Brood of vipers, how
can you speak good, when you are evil?" In all the seven woes
of Holy Tuesday he will emphasize their malign influence on
the people. The evil influence of their words is what he inveighs
against here: "By thy words thou shalt be justified, and by thy
words thou shalt be condemned" (12:33-37).

The second part of the discourse (12:38-45) starts with a
challenge from them: "Master, we want to see a sign from you."

A sign. A proof of your claims. In chapter 11 Christ has
already pointed to his credentials. Those? Worthless! Imposture
or the devil's work. Give us a super-sign — a proof in which
our most captious criticism can find no flaw. And he promises it.

> An evil and adulterous generation demands a sign, and
> no sign shall be given it but the sign of Jonas the prophet.
> For even as Jonas was in the belly of the fish three days
> and three nights, so will the Son of Man be three days
> and three nights in the heart of the earth.

Here is the explanation for the post-ascension mission of the
apostles which Christ announces in the seventh woe. They came
to Israel, above all, as witnesses to his resurrection. But his
promise required more from him than that mission. His enemies
had asked to see a proof they could not refute; it was precisely
this that he promised. And this accounts for the guards-at-the-
tomb theme of the resurrection story. "We remember," the
leaders tell Pilate, "how that impostor said, while he was yet
alive, 'After three days I will rise again.'" They can refer only
to this promise in chapter 12. The prediction they remember
had to be a public one; since there was none such in Mark,
it had to be a Matthean one; and this is the only Matthean one.

When the guards bring them the proof the leaders themselves
have made irrefutable, will they accept it? No.

> The Ninevites will rise up in the judgment with this
> generation and will condemn it; for they repented at the

teaching of Jonas, and behold, a greater than Jonas here. By its rejection of Jonas' anti-type the nation will arrive at its final state of guilt:

> When the unclean spirit has gone out of a man, he roams through waterless places seeking rest and finds none. Then he says, "I will return to my house which I left"; and when he comes to it, he finds it vacant, swept, and set in order. Then he goes and takes with him seven more spirits more evil than himself, and they enter in and dwell there; and the last state of that man becomes worse than the first. So shall it be with this evil generation also.

Israel before Christ's mission to it was like a man possessed, like a house usurped. Christ had come to rescue the man, to reclaim the house — for it was his. Israel was his dwelling place, his temple. Surveying the results of that mission now, what did he see? He had expelled the demon; he had cleansed the house and put it in order. But he could not dwell in it, because the nation would not receive him. So he abandoned it, and the seven-fold guilt of its rejection of him was added to its previous guilt.

That, divested of the figurative wrappings, is what Christ's words mean. They explain the sort of rescue he will have in mind when he says to the nation, "How often I wanted to gather thy children together, as a hen gathers her young under her wings, and thou wouldst not!" They explain the consequences of the abandonment to which he will doom it when he says, "Your house is left to you empty." Those seven maledictions of Holy Tuesday — what are they but the seven devils of guilt that enter Israel as he leaves?

The Matthean additions to the usurped-house discourse, we observe, perform a common function. They clarify the sentence that Christ will pronounce on the Jewish nation in the third part of the Matthean temple discourse.

The discourse in parables in chapter 13 describes the messianic kingdom. Its Matthean and Marcan versions grow from diverse backgrounds. The Matthean grows from the thesis of the Jewish people's rejection by God and the kingdom's transfer to the Gentiles. That thesis is Matthean. Only Matthean insertions state it in the first gospel, and it is conspicuously absent in the second. It is the hinge on which their temple discourses turn. In Mark Christ condemns the leaders, not the people; and the discourse ends with the idyllic episode of the widow's mites. In Matthew he condemns the people together with the leaders; and the discourse ends in a sundering of relations and the most tremendous climax in biblical literature.

The same silence about the Jewish people's rejection prevails in the Marcan counterpart of the plowed-up area. It has no cure of the centurion's slave, with the prophecy of the kingdom's transfer that went with it. It has no reply to John's disciples, with the condemnation of "this generation" that followed it. And the Marcan version of the usurped-house discourse condemns only the Jewish leaders. How the second gospel will paint the future of the kingdom is therefore predictable.

When Jesus explains why he teaches in parables, he quotes an Isaian prophecy (Is 6:9), announcing the Jewish people's rejection. It is "those outside" who are rejected — not the Jewish people — in Mark's version of that prophecy: "To those outside," Christ says, "all things are treated in parables, that '*Seeing they may see, but not perceive; and hearing they may hear, but not understand; lest perhaps at any time they should be converted, and their sins be forgiven them*" (Mk 4:12).

But here is the Matthean version:

> To you it is given to know the mysteries of the kingdom of heaven but to them it is not given. For to him who has shall be given, and he shall abound; but from him who does not have shall be taken away even that which he has. This is why I speak to them in parables, because seeing they do not see, and hearing they do not hear, nor do they understand. In them is fulfilled the

prophecy of Isaias, who says, *"Hearing you will hear, but not understand; and seeing you will see, but not perceive. For the heart of this people has grown hard; their ears they have stopped and their eyes they have shut; lest at any time they see with their eyes and hear with their ears and understand with their mind, and be converted, and I heal them."*

In the Matthean parables on the kingdom, we can see, its transfer to the Gentiles will be stressed; and in the Marcan that transfer will be invisible.

The Marcan discourse (Mk 4:2-33) contains three "seed" parables along with some explanatory and hortatory matter. The first parable is that of the sower; its explanation by Christ reveals that the seed in the good ground is his faithful followers; it is the nascent kingdom whose future unfolds in the second and the third seed parables. The second teaches that this nascent kingdom, like a seed once sown, will grow by its innate divine power till the harvest at the end of the world. The third (the mustard seed) adds that it will grow from tiny beginnings to the grandeur that had been prophesied for it.

In both those parables the kingdom grows up where it was originally planted. No new milieu is foreseen for it.

The Matthean discourse (13:3-52) has a clause after it ("When Jesus had finished all these parables") that tells us it is presented as a unified speech. It begins with the Marcan parable of the sower. The nascent kingdom, as in Mark, consists of Christ's faithful followers. Its future is depicted in two triads of parables.

Why two? We could answer, because two passages deal with the kingdom's transfer in the parable of the marriage feast. Then when asked why two passages deal with the transfer in the marriage feast, we could respond, because they summarize the two triads. We must go deeper, therefore, and say there are two triads because the author stresses not merely a change in the kingdom but also two aspects of it that do not change: its heredity and its basic law. Its members are still the seed that was promised to Abraham, Isaac, and Jacob. Its law stays what it always was — the greatest and first commandment, from which the second is indivisible.

What the parables explain, then, is the Matthean thesis as it was stated in chapter 8: "Many will come from the east and the west and will feast with Abraham and Isaac and Jacob in the kingdom of heaven, but the children of the kingdom will be cast forth into the darkness outside."

Explicit in that thesis is the kingdom's transfer. Implied is its continued radication in the patriarchs. Implied too is the fact that it already existed in their time, and, consequently, that its fundamental law existed as well.

Each triad has one long parable and two short twins. The long ones, which are identical (the wheat-and-cockle = the net), explain the new features of milieu and membership that are caused by the kingdom's transfer. The two pairs of twins (mustard seed and leaven, treasure and pearl) describe its continuing features: its spiritual heredity and its law.

The first triad restates this passage in the parable of the marriage feast:

> (The king) said to his servants, "The marriage feast is ready but those who were invited were unworthy; go therefore to the crossroads and invite to the marriage feast whomever you find." His servants went out into the roads and gathered all whom they found, both good and bad; and the marriage feast was filled with guests.

We see two pictures there: the exodus of the servants to the crossroads of the world; and the hall filled with good and bad guests — the Gentile church, a far cry from the elite Judean church of the first days. Those two pictures return in reverse order in the first triad.

The wheat-and-cockle parable, the Matthean replacement for the Marcan seed-unwatched that grew by its divine power till the harvest at the end of the world, also depicts a seed that grows till that final consummation. But it is a good and a bad seed intermingled — a far cry from that intensely fruitful seed-in-good-ground which Christ the Sower sowed in the first parable. Here "a man" (Christ) sows good seed in "his field." That field, he explains, is the Cosmos — the world. Thus the king's hall full of good and bad guests is transformed into Christ's field full of good and bad seed.

The new features, of milieu and membership, caused by the kingdom's transfer, stand forth in sharp relief.

The continuing element in the membership is contributed by those faithful servants whom the king dispatched to the cross-roads in the parable of the marriage feast. These return in the first triad as the mustard seed. The Marcan parable is subtly altered. In Mark the mustard seed is not transferred from one place to another. In Matthew "a man" *takes it and plants it* in "his field." The same man, obviously, and the same field as in the previous parable. Christ and the world. The servants sent out by the king to the crossroads have been transformed into the good seed that Christ takes and plants in the Gentile world. There, however, it is to grow into the great messianic tree of the kingdom. Thus the kingdom, through that Jewish seed from which it grows will be the kingdom promised to the patriarchs. But how? The parable of the leaven, twin to that of the mustard seed, explains.

A woman takes this leaven and buries it in three measures (an enormous mass) of flour. There it loses its identity but communicates its spirit to the dough. So it will be with those faithful Jewish followers whom Jesus sends to the Gentile world. The outward Jewish features of their faith will disappear, but they will communicate to the Gentile church the spirit they have themselves received from Christ.

Our author rounds off the first triad by telling us that its doctrine is a new revelation, unknown in the Old Testament:

> All these things Jesus spoke to the crowds in parables
> ... that what was spoken through the prophet might be
> fulfilled, "I will open my mouth in parables, I will utter
> things hidden since the foundation of the world"
> (13:34 ff.).

The second triad envisages this other passage in the parable of the marriage feast:

> The king went in to see the guests and he saw there a man who had not on a wedding garment. . . . The king said to the attendants, "Bind his hands and feet and cast him forth into the darkness outside, where there will be the weeping and the gnashing of teeth."

The required wedding garment is the symbol of the kingdom's basic law, which will be enforced when the king enters at the end of the world. The parable of the net describes the enforcement of the law, and the expulsion of the evil into the fire, "where there will be the weeping and gnashing of the teeth." The law itself is stated in the parable of the treasure and the pearl. The simple, comprehensive law, that to possess the kingdom a man must "sell all he has." To love God with *all* one's mind and heart and will and strength — this is the greatest and the first commandment. And it is an *old* doctrine — the one, in fact, from which hangs the whole Law and the prophets.

"Have you understood all these things?" Christ asked them. They said to him, "Yes."

And he said to them, "So every scribe instructed in the kingdom of heaven is like a householder who brings forth from his storeroom things new and old."

Things new — the revelation in the first triad. Things old — the doctrine of the second.

The doctrine of the kingdom's continuity was of vital importance to the Judean church, distressed by the divine sentence rejecting Israel and transferring the kingdom to the Gentiles. We have only to recall Paul's anguish expressed in chapter 9 of his epistle to the Romans. Remembering this, let us turn back to the passage preceding the two triads, in which the apostles' authority is emphasized.

The inner group to whom Christ explains the parables in Mark is "those who were with him and the Twelve." In Matthew that inner group is the Twelve alone: "the disciples came up and asked him."[3] It is they to whom Christ "confided the mysteries of the kingdom." It is they to whom he says:

> Blessed are your eyes, because they see; and your ears, because they hear. For, amen I say to you, many prophets and just men have longed to see what you see and have not seen it; and to hear what you hear and have not heard it (13:16 ff.).

3. Our author had singled out the apostles in the same way of a little earlier. At the end of the usurped-house discourse Christ's mother and brethren call for him. Here is the Marcan account of his response: "A **crowd was sitting about him,** . . . and looking around on **those who were sitting about him,** he said, 'Behold my mother and my brethren'" (Mk 4:32-34). In Matthew, on the contrary, Jesus eliminates the crowd: "Stretching forth his hand to **his disciples,** he said, 'Behold my mother and my brethren'" (Mt 12:49).

6

AN HYPOTHESIS

Our survey of the plowed-up area is now complete. What has emerged from it first of all is the correspondence of its three sections to the three parts of the temple discourse.

Its first section (the sermon on the mount) corresponds to the second part (the instruction) of the temple discourse.

Its second section (Christ's review of his credentials) corresponds to Christ's review of his mission in the first part (the three parables) of that discourse.

The usurped-house discourse corresponds to the third part of that discourse.

The discourse in parables corresponds to two passages in the parable of the marriage feast.

This correspondence, reaching down everywhere to details, cannot be accidental. The plowed-up area does have a unified function. The writer intended it and the temple discourse to be complementary pieces in his design. He intended it to elaborate or explain the themes summed up in the discourse. They form the body and the conclusion of his argument.

The plowed-up area looks to the temple discourse. The temple discourse looks to Christ's departure. That departure, therefore, in which the author saw the apostles' final departure from Jerusalem, was what he had in mind throughout the plowed-up area and the temple discourse. It was the subject he discussed.

With whom? With the Judean church, since he embedded the discussion in a gospel addressed, as the sermon on the mount proves, to that church.

He seems to have addressed it to them as a message from the apostles. We originally based that hypothesis on his identification of the departing Christ with the departing apostles at the end of the temple discourse. It seemed reasonable that the parting words he tied to that departure should be the apostles' valedictory. To confirm that hypothesis we needed a repeated stress by him elsewhere on the apostles' authority to speak in Christ's name. So, proceeding to the plowed-up area, we found in it two instructions (the one in the sermon on the mount and the one in the latter half of chapter 10) specifically addressed to the Judean church; we also found a third (the doctrine of the two triads of parables) which had a surpassing interest for that church.

The first of the three instructions is preceded by a Matthean world. The second is both preceded and followed by Matthean passages stressing the authority of the Twelve. The third is preceded by the Matthean passage in which the mysteries of the kingdom are confided by Christ to them alone.

It seems, then, that the writer designed his discussion of the apostles' departure as a message from them to the Judean church. Indeed, as their farewell message, since it is summed up in the temple discourse, which is itself summed up in the farewell to Jerusalem at the end.

The apostles, as the writer sees them, are in the process of departure to the Gentile world. Where, precisely, does he locate them when they are giving this farewell message? They have left Jerusalem — this is stated at the gospel's close. Yet, since they are in the process of departure, they have not reached their journey's end. They have not yet arrived, it would seem, in the Gentile world. Apparently, then, the writer sees them, when they send their message, in the situation he leaves them in at the end— in Galilee, invested with their world mission and poised to set forth with Christ's omnipotent aid attending them.

Consider the structure of the message. It has the form of an official document sent as a letter. That form, universally used in the old Mediterranean civilization, is still employed by the Holy See and can be observed in any papal encyclical. First came a *praescriptio,* then the message, then the *postscriptio.* The *praescriptio* named the sender of the message, stating his authority; it also named the addressees, usually complimenting them; frequently also it announced the contents of the message. A recent encyclical has this *praescriptio*: "Paul VI, by divine providence Pope, to our venerable brothers, the Patriarchs, Primates, . . . on the doctrine and worship of the Holy Eucharist. Venerable brothers and dear sons, health and apostolic benediction."

At the end of the document came the *postscriptio,* stating the place and date of its sending. The encyclical just alluded to ends thus: "Given at Rome, at St. Peter's, the 3rd day of September, 1965, the third year of our pontificate. Paul VI Pope."

Since the Matthean message is put in Christ's mouth, it should begin with the sermon on the mount, where Christ first "opens his mouth" to teach. More precisely, it should begin with the instruction in that sermon; only from that point on is the discussion summarized in the temple discourse. The beatitudes and the salute to the apostles seem therefore to lie outside the message. They are intimately connected with it nevertheless, since they are the first words that Christ speaks. The writer has given them some function, then, connected with his message. What is it?

The salute to the apostles presents the senders of the message and states their authority: they are Christ's prophets, commissioned by him to illumine the world.

The beatitudes, addressed to the Judean church, present the addressees of the message with compliments, praising their blessedness, which starts with the poverty they chose "in the Spirit" and is crowned by their share in the persecution endured by the apostles. The beatitudes also list the contents of the message: the "justice" of the kingdom in its various aspects (poverty, gentleness, purity of heart, etc.) and the "mysteries of the kingdom" which justify the departure of the apostles.

The beatitudes and the salute to the Twelve thus correspond exactly to the *praescriptio* of an ancient letter.

The message ends with the farewell of the temple discourse. But that discourse lays down the blueprint of a resurrection story; this story, coming at the end of the gospel, has consequently an intimate relation to the message — and some important function connected with it. What is that function?

The story records the arrival of the event — the departure of the apostles — that was discussed in the message. That event has arrived through the operation of the two causes predicted for it. But what was the use of telling the Judean church *that?* Did they need anyone to tell them that the apostles had left? The resurrection story, however, did not stop at the departure of the apostles from Jerusalem; it took them a little further — to Galilee, where they were commissioned to go forth to the Gentile world. There it stopped. It did not mention their exodus to the crossroads of the world, which was also mentioned in the temple discourse. It stopped on the Galilean mountain. *That* gave the addressees of the message important information. It gave them the place and date of its sending.— And the writer had been at pains to make that same scene and situation the setting in which Christ opened his mouth to begin the message.

The Matthean resurrection story therefore corresponds to the *postscriptio* of an official document sent as a letter.

It seems, then, that the writer designed his discussion of the apostles' departure not merely as a farewell message from them to the Judean church, but also as an official document.

If this hypothesis is correct, the Matthean innovations in the remaining areas of the gospel should support it. Insertions preceding the sermon on the mount should announce the message. Those in the other areas should reiterate it. None should contradict it.

7

THE END IN THE BEGINNINGS

The Matthean matter previous to the sermon on the mount should, according to our hypothesis, announce the message of the departing apostles to the Judean church. The writer starts to use Mark in chapter 3; his first two chapters are the purely Matthean infancy story. This large addition at the threshold of his work should play some role in its special design. Between Joseph's settling in Nazareth, where chapter 2 ends, and the first sentence of chapter 3 lies a gap of thirty years. This gap suggests that the connection of his infancy story with the later action is not on the narrative level but on that of exposition. It is a prologue whose role is to adumbrate design.

The story has a title (1:1), a genealogy (1:2-17), and two incidents. Since those incidents contain the bulk and the main interest of the story, they are probably the chief means by which its role is performed.

The title, which replaces the Marcan "Beginning of the good news of Jesus Messias" (Mk 1:1), reads: "Book of genesis of Jesus Messias, son of David, son of Abraham."

"Book of genesis" looks backward and forward. Backward to the title of the first book of the Old Testament, also to Gen 5:1; "Book of genesis of Adam. . . ." Forward to Christ's description of the messianic age in Mt 19:28 as a *new* genesis (*palingensis*): "In the new beginning, when the Son of Man sits on the throne of his glory." That age, starting (Mt 26:64) with Christ's death and resurrection, will be, like the first beginning, for the whole human race. Thus the first Matthean alteration in the Marcan title announces Christ's world mission.

The second addition, "son of David, son of Abraham," seems to reinforce that universalism. "Son of Abraham" would be otiose after "son of David" if the writer wished merely to record Christ's descent. Probably, then, he presents him as that "seed of Abraham" (Gen 22:18), in whom all the nations of the earth were to be blessed. Thus the note sounded in the title's first and last words is universal. Why does the writer call Jesus "son of David"? It was a popular title of the Messias (Mt 12:23; 24:42); whether he had further reasons is conjectural.

The genealogy starting from Abraham presses home the point that Christ is that seed in which the human race was to be blessed. The names in the genealogy include those of four women. Why? No thematic pattern into which they all fit has ever been found.[4] There is, however, one thing they have in common; each name calls up the memory of an intensely human story; each injects life into the long roll-call of empty names. Perhaps this is their function. The writer, as his powerful climax to the temple discourse shows, was not insensible to points of style.

His four mentions of the "transmigration of Babylon" are another matter. The last two are unnatural; displacing the name Jechonias, they become part of the genealogy: "From Abraham to David are fourteen generations, from David to *the transmigration of Babylon* are fourteen generations, from *the transmigration of Babylon* to Christ fourteen generations." This summation shows that for the writer his genealogy has only three points of interest. Abraham, because Jesus was the

4. The four women are Thamar, Rahab, Ruth, and Bethsabee. These supposedly common aspects have been discovered in them: (a) They were all sinners.— But Ruth was not a sinner. (b) They were all Gentiles.— But the biblical accounts do not say that Thamar or Bethsabee was a Gentile. (c) They were all misunderstood women who were later rehabilitated.— But there is no evidence that Rahab, Ruth, and Bethsabee were misunderstood.

promised Seed. David, because Jesus was the Christ. And the transmigration of Babylon — why? Apparently the destruction of Jerusalem and scattering of the Jewish nation also adumbrates a theme in the writer's design.

The two incidents that have the main role in the infancy story play it unequally. The first, recounting the conception and birth of Jesus, has eight verses and little color or drama. The second, the Magi story, is three times as long, is full of color and drama, and concludes the prologue. Obviously, it holds the writer's main interest. He makes it the climax of the prologue, subordinating to it all that precedes.

The first incident is linked with Christ's first title, "son of David." The angel addresses Joseph by that title. In his account the writer seems intent chiefly on the parallel he sets forth between the angel's prophecy and the Isaian, and with the interchangeability thereby implied of the two names, Jesus and Emmanuel:

> "She shall bring forth a son and thou shalt call his name Jesus, because he shall save his people from their sins." Now all this was done that what was spoken by the Lord through the prophet might be fulfilled, "... (she) shall bring forth a son and they shall call his name Emmanuel, which means 'God is with us'" (1:21-23).

The name Jesus signified Christ's salvific mission; the other announced the miraculous signs that proved him incarnate God. His mission and miracles together will be the credentials Christ points to. They are a major theme of the writer's message.

But they are not the subject of that message. The subject — the event it discusses — is Christ's departure, in the person of his apostles, to the Gentile world. And that event is what the second incident, related to Christ's second title, "son of Abraham," adumbrates.

It tells of the infant Christ's flight with his protectors from a murderous attack planned by Herod ... of Gentile eagerness to come to Jesus and do him homage as the messianic king, while the Jewish leaders and people remained apathetic to his coming ... of a miraculous rescue by an angel's nocturnal intervention followed by a nocturnal flight to the Gentile world ... and of a return from that world to the Jews only at a time decreed by God, after those who had sought Christ's life were dead.

This story blends two sets of associations. One set — the contrast of eager Gentile faith with Jewish apathy and disbelief, the murderous attack compelling Christ's protectors to flee, and the return of Christ to the Jews only after his enemies are dead — ties it to the Matthean message about the apostles' departure. The other set — the name, Herod, of the persecuting king, the nocturnal rescue through an angel's intervention, and the nocturnal flight to the Gentile world — connect it with the account of Peter's flight in Acts 12, the event we have fixed on as the probable occasion of the apostles' departure. The story seems, therefore, both to adumbrate the event discussed in the writer's message, and to tie it to Peter's flight.

Between the infancy story and the sermon on the mount John preaches and baptizes Jesus, Jesus is tempted, he comes into Galilee to proclaim the kingdom, and he calls his first four disciples. Those incidents are Marcan; all four have Matthean insertions.

In the Marcan account John does not threaten the Jewish leaders with the transfer of the kingdom and the doom of the Jewish nations. In our first gospel he does:

> When he saw many of the Pharisees and Sadducees coming to his baptism, he said to them, "Brood of vipers! who has shown you how to flee from the wrath to come? Bring forth therefore fruit befitting repentance, and do not think to say within yourselves, 'We have Abraham for our father,' for I say to you that God is able out of these stones to raise up children to Abraham. For even now the axe is laid to the root of the tree; every tree

therefore that is not bringing forth good fruit is to be cut down and thrown into the fire.... His winnowing fan is in his hand and he will thoroughly cleanse his threshing floor, and will gather his wheat into the barn; but the chaff he will burn with unquenchable fire" (3:4-10 and 12).

Here, confronting John, is the league of Pharisees and Sadducees that will confront Jesus in the temple. Here are the strong words ("Brood of vipers!...") that Jesus will use then. Here is his Holy Tuesday demand for fruits. Here impends the double punishment he will then impose for the refusal of the fruits: the transfer of the kingdom (spiritually continuous, however, in spiritual children of Abraham) and the destruction of the fruitless tree. Thus our writer has announced his message in the terms that will sum it up in his temple discourse.

He inserts this passage into the account of Jesus' baptism:

John was for hindering him and said, "I ought to be baptized by thee, and dost thou come to me?" But Jesus answered, "Let it be so now, for it thus befits us to perform all justice" (3:14 ff.).

In the instruction that will come a little later, on the "justice" of the kingdom, Jesus emphasizes that this justice must be performed down to its least details; its teachers will be rewarded if they also do it; teaching without doing is not enough. So here before teaching "all justice" Jesus does it. The writer announces in this insertion the theme of his first instruction to the Judean church.

From his baptism Jesus goes to the desert for his encounter with Satan. Mark barely broaches that topic:

He was in the desert forty days and forty nights, being tempted meanwhile by Satan, and was with beasts, and the angels ministered to him (Mk 1:12 ff.).

Our author, discarding the beasts, builds the temptations up to a memorable climax, wherein Jesus is transported from Jerusalem to a mountain with a view of all the kingdoms of the world. Kingdoms that Satan will grant him on Satan's terms, but that Jesus proposes to conquer by dethroning him. In this climactic scene already looms the mountain at the gospel's close, where Jesus after his victory gives his apostles all the nations of the earth to teach and rule. If that mountain at the end conveys the date and place of the writer's message, he has given a first hint of them on the mountain of temptation.

Jesus now launches into his personal mission. In Mark's words,

> Jesus came into Galilee, preaching the gospel of the kingdom of God and saying, "The time is fulfilled and the kingdom of God is at hand. Repent and believe in the good news" (Mk 1:14 ff.).

After the word "Galilee" in that passage, our author inserts these words:

> And abandoning the town of Nazareth, he came and dwelt in Capharnaum, which is by the sea, in the territory of Zabulon and Nephthalim, that what was spoken through Isaias the prophet might be fulfilled: "Land of Zabulon and land of Nephthalim, by the way to the sea beyond the Jordan, Galilee of the Gentiles: the people who sat in darkness have seen a great light; upon those who sat in the region and shadow of death a light has risen" (4:13-16).

Here, too, the writer seems to be hinting the occasion of his message, for he gives to Jesus' act the features of the apostles' situation at the gospel's close. Jesus has *abandoned* (such is the connotation of the Greek verb) his native town and has gone to the Gentile frontier to fulfill the prophecy about the evangelizing of the Gentiles. So, too, at the end of the gospel the apostles have abandoned their nation and gone to Galilee in order to carry out Christ's mandate to evangelize the Gentiles.

Having now surveyed the Matthean matter that precedes the sermon on the mount, we can draw some conclusions. It consists of a prologue and four insertions. The prologue announces in its title Christ's world mission; its genealogy sounds the Matthean theme of the Jewish nation's doom; its first incident introduces the Matthean theme of Christ's credentials; and its second adumbrates the subject of the writer's message — the transfer of the kingdom — doing this in terms that connect the transfer both with the writer's message and with Acts 12. The first of the four insertions announces his message in terms of his temple discourse. The second announces the theme of his first instruction. The third and fourth seem to hint the place and date of his message.

He has done in this part of his work, therefore, what our hypothesis predicted he would do.

8

THE END IN THE MIDDLE

In the middle area of the gospel (Mt 14:1-21:18; Mk 6:14-11:26) lie four concentrations of Matthean matter and some isolated insertions. If our hypothesis is sound, they will preponderantly repeat themes of the writer's message. None will contradict it.

His first insertion tells how Peter walked the waves at night and was rescued from death.

> Peter answered, "Lord, if it is thou, bid me come to thee over the water." And he said, "Come." Peter got out of the boat and walked on the water to come to Jesus. But seeing the wind was strong, he was afraid; and when he began to sink he cried out, "Lord, save me!" Jesus at once stretched forth his hand and took hold of him, saying, "O thou of little faith, why didst thou doubt?" (14:28-31).

Since this insertion seems connected with the Petrine promise in chapter 16, we shall discuss it there.

His next insertion is in the discourse of 15:1-20 (Mk 7:1-23); from which he omits, let us note, the Marcan parenthesis (Mk 7:3 ff.) explaining Jewish customs. The explanation implies Gentile readers; its omission in Matthew implies Jewish readers. Here is the writer's insertion:

His disciples came up and said to him, "Dost thou know that the Pharisees are scandalized at hearing this saying?" He answered, "Every plant that my heavenly Father has not planted will be rooted up. Don't mind them; they are blind guides of blind men. When the blind lead the blind, both fall into a pit" (15:12).

Reiterated there is the Matthean theme of Pharisaic mis-leadership, disastrous to the Jewish people. "Blind guides" will be echoed in the third and fourth woes of Holy Tuesday.

The story of the Canaanite woman (15:21-28) has two brief insertions. Jesus in the first explains why he does not answer her: "I was not sent except to the lost sheep of the house of Israel." This revives our memory of the apostles' mission to those sheep in chapter 10 — and the post-ascension mission that our author superimposed on it. The other insertion, Christ's praise of the woman's faith, recalls his earlier praise of a Gentile's faith in chapter 8, and the prediction of the kingdom's transfer that went with it.

The first concentration of Matthean matter occurs in chapter 16 (1-20). In the corresponding section of Mark (Mk 8:10-30), Christ clashes with the Pharisees, goes to the Gentile world, near Caesarea Philippi, and has a dialogue there with the Twelve. Our author binds those three incidents together and transforms them into an image of the kingdom's transfer from the Jews to the Gentiles. The clash becomes a final clash with the Jewish leaders, ending in a final break. His journey becomes the continuation of his act of abandonment to its goal in the Gentile world. His dialogue becomes a device for proclaiming there the establishment of the kingdom, his ever victorious Church. That jubilant proclamation, moreover, rings with overtones that relate it to Peter's flight, as recorded in Acts 12. Thus the writer's innovations project not merely an image of the kingdom's transfer, but also of the circumstances in which it will take place.

There is nothing final in the Marcan clash.

The Pharisees came forth and began to dispute with
him, demanding a sign from heaven to test him. Sighing
deeply in spirit he said, "Why does this generation
demand a sign? Amen I say to you, a sign shall not be
given to this generation." And he left them, and getting
into the boat, crossed the lake (Mk 8:11-13).

This is a skirmish like many before it. What does our author
do with it? First, he adds the Sadducees to the Pharisees and
forges the united front that will face Jesus in the temple. Next,
he changes Christ's groan into a menace of imminent disaster.
He further brands "this generation" as "evil and adulterous"—
just as he had done in chapter 12. He promises it — as he did
then — the sign of Jonas. At the end he *abandons* them, (our
author using the same verb as in chapter 4 when Jesus abandoned
his native town). That abandonment involves "this generation"
together with its leaders.

The Pharisees *and Sadducees* came to him to test
him, and they asked him to show them a sign from heaven.
He answered, "When it is evening you say, 'The weather
will be fair, for the sky is red.' And in the morning you
say, 'It will be stormy today, for the sky is red and lower-
ing.' You know then how to read the face of the sky, but
cannot read the signs of the times! An evil and adulterous
generation demands a sign, and no sign shall be given
it but the sign of Jonas." And he abandoned them and
went away (16:1-4).

He goes straight to the Gentiles. In Mark he *crosses* the lake,
comes to Bethsaida, *takes* a blind man *outside the town* in
order to cure him, *goes out to* the villages of Caesarea Philippi,
and *on the way* he *asks* the Twelve a question. All that intermediate movement is erased in Matthew: "Jesus *went away* . . .
and having come to the parts of Caesarea Philippi, he *asked*. . . ."

Our author's main verbs state the start of the journey and its goal — nothing else. And that goal is the question Christ asks, the answer it provokes from Peter, and the jubilant proclamation that crowns the answer.

In Mark the dialogue sounds like casual conversation, whose main interest for Christ and the writer is the prohibition that it leads to: he said to them, "Who do you say that I am?" Peter answered, "Thou art the Christ." And he strictly charged them to say nothing about him to anyone (Mk 8:29 ff.).

In Matthew, on the other hand, Christ's outburst of joy, unique in the gospel, makes the Petrine promise a major climax, the evident focal point of the writer's interest and design.

> He said to them, "Who do you say that I am?" Simon Peter answered, "Thou art the Christ, the Son of the living God." Jesus answered, "Blessed art thou Simon Bar-Jona, for flesh and blood has not revealed it to thee, but my Father who is in heaven. And I say to thee, that thou art Peter, and upon this rock I will build my Church and the gates of hell will not prevail against it. And I will give thee the keys of the kingdom of heaven; and whatever thou shalt bind on earth shall be bound in heaven, and whatever thou shalt loose on earth shall be loosed in heaven."

Christ's parallel promises — to build his Church on Peter and to give him the keys of the kingdom — identify the kingdom with the Church he will establish. He has gone, thanks to the Matthean innovations, from an apparently final clash with the Jewish leaders and a final abandonment of the Jewish nation, to the Gentile world in order to proclaim there the coming establishment of his victorious Church. Again we have the familiar Matthean patterns: a judgment unto victory, the salvation of the Gentiles.

The Petrine promise tells us more. Taken with the Petrine miracle of chapter 14, it seems to tie the kingdom's transfer to the events of Acts 12. Let us consider the significance of the miracle. Peter, at Christ's invitation, walked the waves with him by night and was miraculously rescued from death. Why was he invited to that privileged companionship? The Petrine promise gives the answer. The miracle and the promise go together; they tell the how and the why of Peter's unique relation to Christ. This relation exists, the promise tells us, for the sake of the Church, which is to be built on Peter as its rock, and is to receive thereby the guarantee of its immortality. The guarantee implies the Church's inseparability from Peter and a supernatural aid to him that will keep him steadfast against the gates of hell — the forces of destruction. The miracle shows him, as a result of that influence, triumphing over the flux and instability of natural forces, and rescued from imminent death.

The parallels between the miracle and promise on one hand, and the events of Acts 12 on the other, are these: In Acts 12 Peter is assailed as leader and rock of the Church; that is why his arrest caps the Herodian persecution. The Church remains inseparable from him; "prayer was being made to God for him by the Church without ceasing." Then comes the nocturnal rescue from imminent death, as Christ extends his hand: "Now I know for certain," Peter says, "that the Lord has sent his angel to rescue me." The gates of death do not prevail: "They came to the iron gate ... which opened of its own accord." And there is jubilation in the Church, starting with the little portress who goes almost mad with joy as Peter goes forth to build the Church in the Gentile world.

Chapter 17 has three Matthean insertions. The first identifies the Baptist with Elias, and his betrayers with the Scribes — who will deal in like manner with Jesus:

> "Elias has come already and (the Scribes) did not know him, but did to him whatever they wished. So also shall the Son of Man suffer at their hands." Then the disciples understood that he had spoken to them of John the Baptist (17:11-13).

Those words recall Chapter 11 and Christ saying of John, "If you are willing to receive it, he is Elias who is to come"; and, "From the days of John the Baptist until now the kingdom of heaven suffers violence." He was then, we remember, condemning "this generation" for its rejection of his credentials.

The next insertion, mentioning a mustard seed, recalls the parable of chapter 13, with its revelation of the kingdom's transfer:

> Because of your little faith (you could not expel the demon); for, amen I say to you, if you have faith like a mustard seed, you will say to this mountain, "Move away," and it will move away. And nothing will be impossible to you (17:19).

The third insertion is a new Petrine miracle (17:23-26). In performing it Jesus again associates Peter with himself and miraculously rescues him from the harassment of Christ's enemies. Thus it recalls the earlier Petrine passages and their association with the transfer of the kingdom.

The second concentration of Matthean matter comes in the instruction of chapter 18, which builds on a Marcan original (Mk 9:32-49). The writer omits from it two Marcan passages (Mk 9:37-40 and 49-50), adds a long passage of his own (18:10-35), and at the end imposes unity on the discourse by his transition formula, "When Jesus had brought all these words to a close...."

The Matthean addition has a central part flanked by two parables. These, the lost sheep and the unmerciful servant, return to those great themes of the sermon on the mount, "You are brothers ... and one is your Father, who is in heaven"— as the instruction in the temple discourse will sum them up. The lesson taught by the lost sheep is, "It is not the will of your Father in heaven that one of these little ones should perish." That of the unmerciful servant is, "So also my heavenly Father will do to you, if you do not each forgive your brothers from your hearts." Here is the core of the central passage:

> If he refuses to hear them, appeal to the Church, and
> if he refuses to hear the Church, let him be to thee as
> the Gentile and the publican. Amen I say to you, what-
> ever you bind on earth shall be bound in heaven; and
> whatever you loose on earth shall be loosed in heaven.
> I say to you further, that if two of you shall agree on earth
> about anything for which they ask, it shall be done for
> them by my Father in heaven. For where two or three
> are gathered together in my name, there am I in the
> midst of them (18:17-20).

As the Gentile and the publican. Those words tell us the
instruction was addressed to the Judean church. In every such
instruction preceding it the writer stressed the authority of the
apostles; he does the same here with "Whatever you bind . . .
shall be bound . . . whatever you loose . . . shall be loosed." This
formula, along with the second mention of the Church, and
the omnipotence promised to the Church's prayer, recall the
Petrine promise of chapter 16, and its associations with the
transfer of the kingdom.

Matthew 19:10-12, an insertion counseling virginity, fits into
no pattern we have seen thus far or will see later; it seems to
lie outside the writer's special design — an isolated doctrine he
thought important enough to attach to Christ's teaching on
marriage.

His third concentration comes at the middle and at the end
of a Marcan passage (Mk 10:28-30). At the end he adds the
long parable of the laborers in the vineyard, which is an instruction to the Judean church. In the middle, preceding it, he had
put (as we might expect) a passage stressing the authority of
the Twelve.

> Amen I say to you, that you who have followed me, in
> the new beginning, when the Son of Man shall sit on the
> throne of his glory, shall also sit on twelve thrones, judg-
> ing the twelve tribes of Israel (19:28).

That new beginning, the messianic age, was to commence at Christ's death.[5]

The parable of the laborers in the vineyard deals with the enigmatic Marcan verse, "There are many first who will be last; and last, first" Here is the parable:

> For the kingdom of heaven is like a householder who went out early in the morning to hire laborers for his vineyard. And having agreed with the laborers for a denarius a day, he sent them into his vineyard. And about the third hour he went out and saw others standing in the market place idle; and he said to them, "Go you also into the vineyard, and I will give you whatever is just." So they went. Again he went out about the sixth, and about the ninth hour, and did as before. About the eleventh hour he went out and found others standing about, and he said to them, "Why do you stand here all day idle?" They said to him, "Because no man has hired us." He said to them, "Go you also into the vineyard." When evening came, the owner of the vineyard said to his steward, "Call the laborers and pay them their wages,

5. Christ tells the Jewish leaders on Holy Thursday night, **"From now on,** you will see the Son of Man sitting at the right hand of the Power and coming on the clouds of heaven." In describing the last judgment, it is true, he will also say, "When the Son of Man shall come in his majesty, and all the angels with him, then he will sit on the throne of his glory" (Mt 25:31). Some infer from the parallel between those two passages that Jesus expected the world to end at his death. Whatever this reasoning may be worth, it has no relevance to the present study, which is occupied exclusively with the design of our first gospel. Since this gospel presents a Christ who announces as his main thesis the transfer of the messianic kingdom from the Jews to the Gentiles several years after his death, its insertions are certainly not intended to present a Christ who expected the world to end at his death. The author who made those insertions did not interpret them as the "eschatological school" interprets them, nor did he expect his readers to so interpret them. He must have understood them to mean that the messianic kingdom would begin at Christ's death and reach its consummation with his return long afterwards.

beginning from the last even to the first." When they of the eleventh hour came, they received each a denarius. And when the first in their turn came, they thought they would receive more; but they also received each his denarius. On receiving it, they began to murmur against the householder, saying, "These last have worked a single hour, and thou hast made them equal to us, who have borne the burden of the day and the heat." Answering one of them he said, "Friend, I do thee no injustice; didst thou not agree with me for a denarius? Take what is thine and go. I choose to give to this last even as to thee. Have I not a right to do what I choose? Art thou envious because I am generous?" This is how the last shall be first, and the first last; for many are called, but few are chosen.

The illative "for" at the beginning, and "this is how" at the end, of the parable show that it explains the Marcan verse, though this is not enigmatic when read against the background of the basic Matthean thesis. The "many first," we know from that thesis, are the Jews; and the "many last" who will be first are the Gentiles. The parable deals with the occasion of the kingdom's transfer.

Its first-hour laborers are the Jews, its eleventh-hour laborers are the Gentiles. Who are the middle groups who are ignored in the denouement? They may be stylistic embellishments; or they may represent the Samaritans (see Acts 8). The vineyard is the kingdom. At the eleventh hour it has become the Church of the New Testament; the Gentiles, who enter it then, did not serve the true God earlier. At the first hour it was in the promissory and preparatory stage that began with Abraham.

The cause of Jewish anger is the equal treatment given both Jews and Gentiles in the Church: "You have made them equal to us." This equality of treatment is not the final reward of heaven, which is to be given to each "according to his works" (Mt 16:27). Nor is it God's intermediate rewards; these are given in proportion to each one's cooperation with the graces he has already received (Mt 13:12). It can only be the initial gift of membership that was conferred by baptism and the imparting of the Spirit. The Jews are angered by the admission of Gentiles carrying only the light burden (11:30) of faith, while the Jews bore besides it the intolerable yoke (Acts 15:10) of the Torah and the traditions.

Paying the last arrivals first seems to be a plot mechanism, enabling the first-hour laborers to see what these get and to expect more for themselves. The lesson of the parable lies in their brusk dismissal, "Take what is thine and go," and in Christ's comment thereon: "This is how they will become the last to enter the kingdom."

The admission of the Gentiles into the Church without circumcision, the parable seems to say, will cause the Jews to turn from it in anger. This is what we already inferred from the events of Acts 10 to 12 — from the change in the Jewish people's attitude towards the apostles after Peter received the Gentiles into the Church without circumcision. For the third time, then — as in the Magi story and in the Petrine promise — our author seems to point to Herod Agrippa's persecution as the occasion of the apostles' departure from Jerusalem.

The parable aimed a special warning at the Judean church; it warned that complainers about Gentile equality with themselves might be excluded by God from the kingdom along with the mass of the Jewish nation.

Outside the plowed-up area our author inverts the Marcan order only once; when he puts Christ's cleansing of the temple before the cursing of the fig tree. At this point, too, occurs his next concentration of Matthean matter.

In Mark, Christ enters Jerusalem on Sunday; on Monday he curses the tree and cleanses the temple; and on Tuesday his disciples find the tree withered. In Matthew those four events, thanks to the writer's alterations, become two — an entrance-and-cleansing, and a sentence immediately executed — two symbols that embody his whole message.

Christ dooms the fig tree for not yielding him its fruits, and its life visibly departs; "immediately the fig tree withered up." Proceeding thence to the temple he dooms the Jewish nation for not yielding him its fruits, and at once he, the life of that nation, departs. Thus the writer joins a symbolic act to its explanation, following one of the commonest patterns of divine oracles in the Old Testament. Just so had the prophet Ahias (3 K 11:29-32) torn his cloak into twelve parts, giving Jeroboam eleven, and had then explained his act.

The whole history of Christ's salvific mission to Israel is presented in the first of the two paired symbols, the entrance and cleansing of the temple. Our author had laid the ground for the symbolism in chapter 12. Christ had pictured himself there as a conqueror who drives a usurping demon from a house, which he then cleanses, sets in order — and abandons. This house, the center of Israel, was the temple; and it was Christ's house: "a greater than the temple is here."

Entering that house on Palm Sunday, he asserts his ownership. "My house is a house of prayer," he tells the Jewish leaders, "but you have made it a den of thieves." He cleanses it and sets it in order; then he disowns it. "*Your* house is left to you empty," he tells the nation on Holy Tuesday. And he abandons it.

Since the Matthean version of the Palm Sunday drama thus corresponds to the Matthean picture in the usurped-house discourse, it ought to express the totality of Christ's mission, starting with the Baptist's preaching and closing with that of the apostles after Pentecost. The writer's changes do in fact suggest that total history.

At Christ's entrance, he says, this prophecy of Zachary (Zach 9:9) was fulfilled:

> Tell the daughter of Sion: "Behold, thy king comes to thee, propitious, seated on an ass, on a colt, the foal of a beast of burden."

What Zachary had announced in that oracle was the totality of the messianic mission to Israel.

4

The writer's mention of the commotion in the capital recalls the Magi's coming to Jerusalem with the news that the Messias was in the nation's midst. The coming of the Magi had incited the attack that sent Jesus to the Gentiles; it was a symbol, therefore, of his entire mission to Israel.

Jesus says in Mark, quoting Isaias 56:7, "My house shall be called a house of prayer *for all the Gentiles.*" That last phrase is omitted in Matthew. Its inclusion in Mark and its omission in Matthew are both consistent. Its inclusion conforms to the Marcan pattern of an unrejected Jewish nation, the messianic center to which the Gentiles will be drawn. Its omission fits into the contrary Matthean pattern of a nation that has forfeited its messianic destiny.

The writer's last insertion is this:

> The blind and the lame came to him in the temple, and he healed them. But the chief priests and the Scribes, seeing the wonderful things that he did, and the children crying out, "Hosanna to the Son of David," were indignant and said to him, "Dost thou hear what these are saying?" Jesus said to them, "Yes; have you never read, 'Out of the mouth of infants and sucklings thou hast perfected praise'?" And abandoning them he went out of the city.

That passage stirs echoes. Its miracles and its fulfilled prophecy — those are the credentials Christ pointed to in chapter 11. The chief priests and the Scribes — those are the leaders of the leagued parties that confronted Jesus at the lakeside in chapter 16, as they had confronted John before him at the Jordan. Today he abandons them with a curt answer as he did then, and sets the stage for his next act, the dooming of the fruitless tree.

Thus with two symbols the writer has knotted together his design.

This is what his four concentrations of Matthean matter and his other insertions have done in the area between the parables and the temple discourse: His first concentration conjured up the kingdom's transfer, clothed in adjuncts that pointed to the persecution of Herod Agrippa. His second, an extension of the instruction in the sermon on the mount, was addressed to the Judean church, and, like all such instructions before it, stressed the authority of the apostles. His third, a new instruction to the Judean church, with another passage stressing the apostles' authority, dealt with the transfer of the kingdom and again connected it with Herod's persecution. His fourth converted four Marcan incidents into two symbols that embody his whole message. His other insertions, with but one exception, repeated themes of the message; that exception, the counsel of virginity, lay outside the message but did not contradict it.

Our hypothesis predicted that the writer's innovations in this area would reiterate the themes of the message he wrote into the plowed-up area and the temple discourse. That prediction has been verified.

9

THE AUTHOR COMPLETES HIS CASE

In Mark, Jesus passes to the eschatological discourse over this bridge of incident:

> As he was going out of the temple, one of his disciples said to him, "Master, see what wonderful stones and buildings!" Jesus answered, "Dost thou see all these great buildings? There will not be left one stone upon another that will not be thrown down." And as he was sitting on the Mount of Olives, Peter and James and John and Andrew asked him privately, "Tell us, when are these things to happen, and what will be the sign when all these things will begin to come to pass?"

The ensuing discourse deals with Jerusalem's destruction (Mk 13:5-23) and Christ's return (13:24-37). The last five verses (33-37) warn the disciples to be on the watch for that return.

Our author absorbed this Marcan discourse into his own, except for the passage on Jewish persecution, which he had shifted to chapter 10. He enlarged the Marcan warning into a whole chapter; and at the end he imposed unity on the discourse by the clause, "It came to pass *when Jesus had finished all these words....*" His discourse has, consequently, the same themes as the Marcan; but these grow logically out of what precedes, whereas in Mark they do not.

Jerusalem's destruction implied the Matthean thesis of the Jewish nation's rejection by God. It does not surprise the apostles; they ask only, "When is it to happen?" Apparently the thesis is familiar to them. Yet nowhere in Mark is that thesis found. Its implication in the eschatological discourse puts the discourse outside its Marcan frame. It lays bare something like an inconsistency in Mark.

For Christ's return, the second theme of the discourse, the reader is likewise unprepared. The apostles had not asked about it; and it had no necessary association with the destruction of Jerusalem or the temple; those catastrophes had occurred before without the world's coming to an end.

In Matthew, on the contrary, both themes are apposite. Both answer questions raised by the apostles. Christ's many affirmations of the Matthean thesis have familiarized them with it and was reaffirmed in the solemn sentence he had just pronounced in the temple. His first theme in the eschatological discourse merely elaborates the prediction of Jerusalem's destruction he had made in the parable of the marriage feast. He had spoken, too, of his return — the discourse's second theme — in his farewell to Jerusalem. Hence it was natural for his disciples to ask him when this return would come; and they did so in the Matthean transition. They coupled the question with the Marcan one about the temple: ". . . and what will be the sign of thy coming and of the end of the world?" Thus the Matthean eschatological discourse is the logical sequel, the epilogue, of the Matthean temple discourse.

There are four Matthean insertions in the passion story. The third goes with the second, and the fourth answers the first. The first is these words of Christ at his arrest:

> Put back thy sword into its place; for all who take the sword shall perish by the sword. Or dost thou suppose that I cannot ask my Father and he will immediately furnish me with more than twelve legions of angels? (26:52 ff.).

There at the start of Christ's passion is the Matthean theme of his claim to absolute power as Son of God. At his death a miraculous display of divine power confirms that claim. The display and its effect on Gentile beholders are recorded in the fourth insertion, which we italicize here in its Marcan context:

> The curtain of the temple was torn in two from top to bottom; *and the earth quaked, and the rocks were rent, and the tombs were opened, and many bodies of the saints who had fallen asleep arose; and coming forth out of the tombs after his resurrection, they came into the holy city and appeared to many.* Now, when the centurion, *and those who were with him,* keeping guard over Jesus, *saw the earthquake and the things that were happening, they were much afraid,* and *they* said, "Truly, he was the son of God" (27:51-54).

There, reiterated, are the Matthean themes of Christ's credentials, and of Gentile, not Jewish, readiness to accept them.

The second and third insertions form the familiar Matthean pattern in which the guilt of the Jewish leaders engulfs the Jewish people. The bad faith of the leaders is revealed in their conduct when Judas repents.

> Judas ... brought back the thirty pieces of silver to the chief priests and the elders, saying, "I have sinned in betraying innocent blood." "What do we care?" they said. "That is your business." He flung the money into the temple and went away and hanged himself with a halter. The chief priests took the money and said, "It is not lawful to put it in the treasury; it is the price of blood." After a consultation they bought with it the potter's field as a burial ground for strangers. That is why the field has been called Haceldama, Blood Field, even to this day (27:3-10).

The phrase, "even to this day," does not mean that the writer leaned on an old tradition. It is a prosecutor's phrase. Throughout the gospel he had arraigned the Jewish leaders. Here he pointed to a proof of their guilt which his readers could behold for themselves — the field whose very name told how the authorities had come by it. Just so an attorney in court might point to the estate on which the defendant was living "even to this day" as proof of his guilt.[6]

In the next insertion the Jewish people become entangled in their leaders' guilt. The wife of Pilate begs him to have nothing to do with "this just man" (27:19). Her plea creates suspense about Pilate himself and prepares a dramatic climax. What will he do? He washes his hands before the crowd to protest his innocence. "*The whole people* cried, 'His blood be on us and on our children.'" In describing that Jerusalem mob as "the whole people" the writer completed a Matthean pattern we have seen often before.[7]

Our hypothesis required the Matthean innovations in this area to reiterate the themes of the Matthean message in the plowed-up area and the temple discourse. They have done so. The inserted question preceding the eschatological discourse makes that discourse the epilogue of the temple discourse. The

6. "Even to this day" has the same connotation in Mt 28:15. Again the author is convicting the Jewish leaders on evidence his readers could see for themselves. This time the evidence was the tale they kept assiduously spreading — a tale whose falsehood was branded on its face. No soldiers would declare they had slept at their post; nor could they testify to what had happened while they slept. On the other hand, the tale proved that the tomb had been guarded, and that the soldiers, who had gone unpunished, must have told the leaders a different story which they dared not disclose.

7. This passage has sometimes been abused by being twisted to antisemitic purposes. For this reason we should keep two points of the author's design in mind. One is the disparity he sees between the guilt of the leaders and the guilt of the people they misled. The second is that he sees in the conglomerate of leaders and people, not the Jewish **race**, but only "this generation"— those who had received the messianic mission that started with John and closed when the apostles left Jerusalem.

additions to the passion story repeat those basic themes of the message: the credentials of Jesus as Son of God, their acceptance by Gentiles, and their rejection by his own people.

10

CONCLUSIONS AND A PROBLEM

We have now surveyed the Matthean changes outside of
the plowed-up area, the temple discourse, and the resurrection
story. They were many, and some were massive: an infancy
story and four other concentrations, along with many isolated
passages, big and small. With the exception of the passage on
virginity they have a common feature; they evoke, either announcing or recalling, the themes of the Matthean message
written into the plowed-up area and the temple discourse.
Consistency on such a scale cannot be due to chance; it was
planned. That common feature is the effect those changes were
meant to have. To keep pointing to that Matthean message,
to keep directing the reader to it — this is their function.

Our survey has turned up two additional instructions
addressed to the Judean church, besides the three in the plowed-
up area. Like those three they have companion passages stressing
the authority of the apostles. The consistency of this pattern
with the writer's presentation of the temple discourse as a farewell message from them is another fact that cannot be explained,
it seems, by chance. The writer designed his gospel as their
farewell message to the Judean church.

Three passages (the Magi story, the Petrine promise, and
the laborers in the vineyard), all dealing with the transfer of
the kingdom to the Gentiles, have many parallels to the account
of Herod Agrippa's persecution in the Acts of the Apostles.
Other passages, which we had already seen, in chapter 10 and

in the temple discourse, associate the apostles' departure with a murderous attack on them by the Jewish authorities. The consistency of this pattern with the probability, already established, that the apostles went to the Gentile world because of Herod's persecution, is a third fact that can hardly be explained by chance. That persecution was not merely the probable, it was the certain occasion of their departure.

Two questions remain. Did our first gospel convey a genuine or a spurious message from the apostles? If it was genuine, did an apostle write it, or did a secretary?

Spurious apostolic missives have two marks. They shout their claim to apostolic authority, and they wait till the apostle is safely dead. Both traits are needed for a successful imposture. If they do not shout, they will go unnoticed. If the apostle is alive, he will disown them.

Our first gospel makes no overt claim to apostolic authority. It originally had no title. It starts with no allusion to the apostles. Its design to present itself as apostolic is so unobtrusive that only an exhaustive study discloses it. Lacking this first mark of a spurious message, it must also lack the second. If it appeared at any other time but the crisis caused by the apostles' departure, the author could not expect his design to be noticed; all his toil on it would be wasted. He had to produce it for that crisis, to deal with that crisis and at a time therefore when the apostles were at hand or could be reached, at a time when they could be leaving a genuine message which would unmask any spurious one. Hence our first gospel can hardly be anything else than a genuine apostolic message to the Judean church.

Did an apostle write it? Two small Matthean insertions that we have not yet considered seem to answer that question.

In Mark (2:14-17) the publican whom Christ calls to be an apostle is named Levi. In Matthew (9:9) he is called Matthew.

When our author comes in the Marcan list of the Twelve (Mk 3:18; Mt 10:3) to the name of Matthew, he inserts after it the words, "the publican." His gospel has many rude side-glances (some of them Matthean) at publicans. It couples "publicans and sinners" (9:10; 11:19); "heathens and publicans"

(18:7); "publicans and prostitutes" (21:31). In such a context what apostle would twice alter his source to call attention to a brother apostle's publican background? What secretary of an apostle would do so? Surely it was no one but Matthew himself.

Since those two insertions were the last pieces of evidence we had to examine, our study of the first gospel is now complete. It has led to these conclusions: that Matthew wrote it, acting as spokesman for the other apostles; that he addressed it to the Judean church; that besides being a written reminder of their instructions (its general design), he meant it to serve as a "white paper," justifying their departure to the Gentiles, and exhorting the Judean church to stand firm in the Christian revelation they had taught; and that he wrote it while he, if not the other apostles, was still in Palestine, sometime between 41 and 44 A.D., probably in 42.

How can those conclusions be reconciled with the gospel's dependence on Mark? Our second gospel, it is commonly held, was written in Italy sometime in the sixties. How can a work that used it as a source have been written in the forties? This paradox need not dismay us. Our conclusions about Matthew have been deduced from the complete evidence. The conclusions about Mark are not based on the complete evidence. We must undertake a new examination of the second gospel.

11

MARK'S TEXT AND NOTES

We do not begin our study of Mark now; it has been going on, side by side with that of Matthew, from the first chapter of this book. It has uncovered more than one contrast between the two gospels which seems rooted in their contrasting designs. Those contrasts are valuable clues. Another clue is the difference between the parenthetical matter and the principal content — between the "notes" and the "text"— of the second gospel.

Its "notes" comprise the following:

1. An explanation of Jewish ritual washings (Mk 7:3 ff.). This must have been meant for Gentile readers.

2. Nine translations of Aramaic (Hebrew) expressions into Greek (3:17; 5:41; 7:11; 7:34; 9:43; 10:46; 14:36; 15:22; 15:34). Though the second gospel has many more of these translations than any other gospel, they do not help us, since their function may be purely stylistic — to give the "atmosphere" of the milieu in which its action takes place.

3. Four "translations" of *Greek* terms into other Greek terms. These are unexpected and significant. Two of them make intelligible to Gentile readers terms that had a special meaning to Greek-speaking Jews. In 7:2 "common hands" is explained as "unwashed hands"; in 15:42 "preparation" is explained as "sabbath-eve." Those two translations suggest that a text originally meant for Greek-speaking Jews was later adapted for Gentile readers.

The other two suggest that a text originally meant for eastern readers was later adapted for use in the west. One (12:42) explains that two *lepta* (the lepton was a coin used in the eastern regions of the Roman empire) were equal to one *quadrans,* a coin used in the west. The other (15:16) translates *aulē* (used in the east to designate the official residence of a Roman governor) into its Latin equivalent, *praetorium.*

Those four "translations," taken together, suggest that the contents of the gospel were originally intended for Greek-speaking Jews of the east (for instance, those of Judea) and were later adapted for Gentiles of the west.

4. The apparition narrative (16:9-20). Ending with the statement that the apostles "went forth and preached everywhere," it seems to suppose a state of things that did not exist much before 60 A.D.

In their sum, then, the Marcan "notes" indicate that the second gospel was published somewhere in the west for Gentile readers, probably not before 60 A.D. They also indicate that there may have been an earlier edition, without notes, for Greek-speaking Jews of the east.

We turn now to the Marcan "text."

We cannot study the design of the "text" by laying it alongside some earlier work that its author used and altered. We can deduce something, however, from the presence in it of elements that Matthew and Luke omit. We can also draw some inferences from the presence or absence in it of elements that ought to be present or absent in it, given either of two suppositions: that it was intended for Jews or intended for Gentiles.

One pervading type of ingredient found in Marcan passages but dropped by Matthew and Luke when they borrowed them is that of the vivid, irrelevant details which an eyewitness puts into his story to betoken that he *is* an eyewitness. Apparently, then, it was part of the narrator's design to present himself as an eyewitness of the things he relates.

Who was he? Those vivid, irrelevant details crop up in the stories of Jairus' daughter, of the transfiguration, and of the agony of Jesus in Gethsemani, where only Peter, James, and John were present. He was one of those three. They recur in the story of Peter's denials of Christ, (14:54 and 66-70) where Peter was alone. This fact, along with some other peculiarities in the gospel's treatment of Peter, suggests that the narrator is Peter himself.

Now comes the crucial question. Does the "text" record the instructions Peter gave in Jerusalem up to 42 A.D., or those he gave later to the Gentiles? Almost every chapter shows that it is his Jerusalem catechesis.

In the first place he omits — deliberately, it seems — every passage that announces the rejection of the Jews and the election of the Gentiles. We have seen the long list of such passages in Matthew; later we shall see others in Luke. Many occur both in Matthew and Luke — strong evidence that they are authentic logia, which every apostle would know. Let us review them.

Mark opens with the preaching of the Baptist. Into that preaching Matthew puts John's warning of Jewish rejection, Gentile election:

> Do not think to say within yourselves, "We have Abraham for our father"; for I say to you that God is able out of these stones to raise up children to Abraham. . . .

Luke includes that passage. Mark omits it.

In the account of Christ's temptations (Mk 1:13) Matthew records the world vision offered to Jesus from the mountain. Luke has it, too; Mark omits it.

In the house-divided discourse (Mk 3:20-30) Mark implies no doom of the Jewish nation. Matthew gives the solemn passage foretelling the condemnation of "this generation" by the Ninevites and the Queen of the South, and also the passage describing the nation's last state. Luke, too, has those passages.

When Jesus explains (Mk 4:11 ff.) why he resorts to parables, he quotes a prophecy of Isaias denouncing doom on those who are deaf to his preaching. Mark vaguely identifies these as "those outside," and omits the part of the prophecy which identifies them as the Jewish people. Not so in Matthew; there we read: "For the heart of *this people* is hardened. . . ."

Among the Marcan parables there is only one with a Gentile horizon; it is far off, and it seems to be merely the *extension* to Gentiles of a kingdom that is immovably Jewish. This version of the parable of the mustard seed is not the one we find in Matthew and Luke (Luke 13:18-21). There implied, and openly asserted in the companion parable of the leaven, is the announcement of the *transfer* of the kingdom to the Gentiles.

The Marcan account of the dispute over Jewish tradition (7:1-23) gives no hint that the people are doomed. In Matthew we find this dialogue, which seems germane to the dispute:

> His disciples said to him, "Do you know that the Pharisees were scandalized by this saying?"
>
> He answered, "... Let them alone. They are blind guides of blind men. When the blind guide the blind, both fall into a pit."

The oracular utterance that "the first shall be last, and the last first" (Mk 10:31) needs an explanation. Mark does not give one. Matthew does; it is the parable of the laborers in the vineyard, with its transparent announcement of Gentile election, Jewish rejection.

There is nothing in the Holy Tuesday discourse of Jesus in Mark (12:1-40) that gives any hint of a judgment on the Jewish nation. We remember well what that discourse is in Matthew. But it is worth noting that Luke in a different context has a twin to the parable of the marriage feast (Lk 14:16-24); he has also the seven woes (11:39-52). And Mark omits them.

To these we should add Christ's prophecy of the Gentiles' entering the kingdom and the Jews being cast out, which both Matthew and Luke record (Mt 8:11; Lk 13:28) and Mark omits. Likewise the doom of the Galilean towns found in Matthew and Luke (Mt 11:20-24; Lk 10:12-15), but not in Mark.

To sum up: nowhere in Mark is there a statement that the Jewish people are, or will be, rejected by God for their rejection of Christ. And this total exclusion of all the logia in which their doom is foretold or denounced seems deliberate; for, as we have seen, it leaves in the air, unexplained and inexplicable, the destruction of Jerusalem that Jesus describes in the eschatological discourse. The apostles, in the Marcan account, are not surprised. *They* know why the capital is doomed; and the apostle whose narrative is recorded in Mark has not let *us* know.

Now, the only plausible reason we can give for the deliberate suppression of those logia is that Mark's text records Peter's preaching to the Jews in the years 30-42, when the nation was receiving its "last chance" before the departure of the apostles to the Gentile world. To tell them in those years that they were already rejected, was unthinkable; not to tell the Gentiles later that the kingdom was now transferred to them, was equally unthinkable.

Fortunately, the New Testament furnishes us with samples of Peter's preaching to the Jews during the Jerusalem years, and of his preaching to the Gentiles in his Roman years. We find the former in Acts 1 to 12; the latter in First Peter.[8] When he preaches in Jerusalem he says nothing about a divine rejection of the Jews; no, the promises stand firm, and the Gentiles will someday be included in them only by extension: *"For to you is the promise and to your children* and to all who are far off" (Acts 2:39).

8. The authenticity of First Peter is affirmed by the unanimous voice of the early Church tradition. Irenaeus, Clement of Alexandria, Origen, Tertullian, and Cyprian quote it as Peter's and Eusebius lists it among the uncontroverted sacred writings. The objections to its authenticity are flimsy: (1) The letter implies that Christianity was a proscribed religion, and that its adherents were being persecuted; such a state of things, it is objected, did not arise till the time of Trajan.— The fact is, however, that Christianity became an outlawed religion by Nero's edict of 64 A.D. and remained such till Constantine's Edict of Toleration. The way Roman officials dealt with members of the outlawed creed depended on themselves, except when the emperors issued special directions, as, for instance, Trajan did in his answer to Pliny's inquiry. (2) The author leans on Paul's letters; Peter, it is objected, would not have done so, since Paul was his rival.— But this rivalry is asserted on the flimsiest grounds. (3) The Greek of the letter, it is objected, is better than an unlettered Galilean fisherman could write.— But the author himself says that the letter was drafted by Sylvanus, who, presumably, was the Sylvanus of Acts 16:37, a Jew of the Dispersion and a Roman citizen.

But when he writes to the Gentiles, he tells them that *they* are now God's chosen race, replacing the Jews:

> For you who believe is this honor; but to those who do not believe, "a stone which the builders rejected has become the head of the corner," and "a stumbling block and rock of scandal" to those who stumble at the word and do not believe; for this is also their destiny. You, however, are a chosen race ... (1 Pet 2:7).

An apostle could also be expected, when preaching to Gentiles, to cite the fulfillment of Old Testament prophecies that foretold their salvation. Peter does so. Immediately after the lines we have just quoted, he goes on to quote the Osean prophecy (Os 1:6,9) that has now been fulfilled:

> You who in times past were "not a people" are now the people of God; you who did "not obtain mercy" now have "obtained mercy."

When, on the other hand, he had preached to the Jews in the early years, he had announced no Gentile salvation fulfilling an ancient oracle. The Messias was to be a universal king, who would extend the blessings of his reign to the Gentiles; and twice Peter cited prophecies (Acts 2:17; 3:25) which envision such an extension in some indefinitely remote future; but his visible horizon, when he quotes them, is exclusively Jewish.

Here, then, is another test for the Marcan text. If it records Peter's Jerusalem catechesis, its Gentile horizon should be as indefinitely remote as Peter's was in the early chapters of the Acts before his vision at Joppa jolted him. It should contain no prophecy whose main concern is with Gentile salvation. If the text records a Gentile catechesis, it should contain at least one such prophecy.

Applying the test, what do we find? Not only no such prophecy; but the deliberate (it seems) suppression of one — at the very start of the gospel. The narrator begins with an Isaian oracle which proclaimed universal salvation:

> The voice of one crying in the desert, "Make ready the way of the Lord, make straight his paths. . . ."

There the narrator stops. Luke, who wrote for Gentiles, did not stop. Quoting that same prophecy in the same context (Lk 3:4-6), he gave it all:

> ". . . every valley shall be filled, and every mountain and hill shall be brought low . . . and *all flesh shall see the salvation of God.*"

That contrast between Luke and Mark is devastating.

New evidence that the Marcan text records Peter's Jerusalem catechesis appears in other omissions. It has a habit of broaching vital themes, which it then leaves undeveloped.

Its most glaring omission is the resurrection story. Jesus had made the apostles his official witnesses; witnesses, first of all, of his resurrection. According to Paul's catechesis (1 Cor 15:1-11), which, he says, agreed with the catechesis of the Twelve, Peter was the first apostle to whom Jesus appeared after his resurrection. Peter *had* to testify to that. Moreover, even before this apparition (according to Luke and John), Peter had gone on Easter Sunday morning to the tomb as soon as the women had reported the removal of the stone. He had to tell what he had then found inside the tomb. Finally, if he was preaching in Rome, he had no other apostle with him and must describe *all* the apparitions mentioned by Paul as part of the common catechesis.

The Marcan text has none of all this. It broaches the resurrection story by telling how the women went to the tomb, found the stone rolled away, and were told by an angel that Jesus had risen; and how they fled and said nothing. There the story stops. Why? Some hazard the guess that the last pages of Mark have perished. This seems improbable. In Mark's lifetime copies of his gospel were being used in many churches. The last pages of *all* those copies did not perish; and any church that lost them could easily replace them from the copy of another church. No; there seems to be only one likely explanation for the broached but undeveloped resurrection story of the Marcan text, and for its other broached, undeveloped themes.

The explanation is that the text records the instructions Peter gave when he was the first speaker of the whole apostolic team. The other apostles were not rubber stamps, whose role was simply to stand around and nod assent to what Peter said. They were his peers; and it was but proper to show it by dividing the apostolic catechesis and giving each a share, which the rest confirmed by their presence while he spoke. Since Peter spoke first, his portion was introductory; it was the basis on which the others built, the trunk from which they branched out. Thus, part of its task was to broach themes which the others were to develop. Philip (let us say) dilated on the parables, and Matthew on other discourses of the Lord. Thus, too, where Peter's part stopped, it stopped like the end of a chapter, not like the end of a book. It left the listener in suspense, expecting a continuation. And the next speaker — John, perhaps — picked up the unfinished story of the resurrection.

This peculiarity of the Marcan text, that it looks not like a complete apostolic catechesis, but like the introductory portion, the first of many parts of the whole catechesis, points to the years when the Twelve worked together as a team in Jerusalem, before Herod's persecution dispersed them and sent them to the Gentiles.

Some minor features of the gospel are also suggestive. Though its "notes" clarify passages a Gentile would not understand, he would need more of them. The Baptist, for instance, was unknown to the Gentiles; and the details of his story were probably little known even to Jews outside of Palestine. Keeping in mind that our first gospel was written for Palestinian Jews, and our third for Gentiles, let us see how Matthew, Mark, and Luke deal with John's story.

Mark brings John on stage abruptly without introducing him to the reader. Matthew does the same. Luke does not bring him on stage till he has narrated his background in the infancy story.

Mark casually alludes to John's being "handed over," as if the reader ought to understand the allusion. Matthew does the same. Luke drops the allusion and tells his readers plainly what happened to John (Lk 3:19 ff.).

Mark gives us the dialogue that took place when Jesus and the apostles were coming down from the Mount of the Transfiguration; in it is the logion, unintelligible to a Gentile, that "Elias has already come." Matthew gives the same dialogue and logion. Luke drops the dialogue; he gives instead, in the infancy story, the angel's oracle that John would go before the Messias "in the spirit and power of Elias."

Then there is the debate about unwashed hands, which fills 23 verses in Mark (7:1-23). To Gentile catechumens it had no value; and even with Mark's notes it remained hopelessly obscure.[9] Matthew, too, recounts the debate. Luke drops it.

Those four passages, taken together, and applied to the first three gospels, are like a litmus-paper test. Is Mark's text a catechesis for Jews or for Gentiles? Four times its reaction to the test is that of a catechesis for Jews.

Against the mass of evidence that it records Peter's Jerusalem catechesis — against its total suppression of logia that foretell or denounce the rejection of the Jewish people, its omission of all prophecies of Gentile salvation, its truncated presentation of vital themes that a catechesis for Gentiles ought to elaborate, as well as the passages that served our "litmus-paper" experiment — against all these, is there any counter-evidence in the

9. What, for example, could a Gentile make of this retort of Jesus, even when helped by the writer's translation of **Corban?**

> You say, "If any man says to his father or mother, 'Corban' (which means "gift") 'whatever help you may get from me,' you no longer allow him to do anything for his father or mother, making void the word of God by your tradition" (Mk 7:11-13).

text that points to its being a catechesis for Gentiles? Apparently not. Not even the prohibition of divorce, couched in terms of Gentile law.

When the Pharisees put the question of divorce to Jesus (Mk 10:2-12), they did it in terms of Jewish law, which allowed a husband to divorce his wife, but not vice versa; whereas the law of the Empire, which prevailed even in Gentile parts of Palestine, such as the Decapolis, allowed either partner to divorce the other. Every Jew, therefore, was familiar with both laws. When Jesus answered the question, he universalized it by reverting to the marriage law that God had laid down for the human race in the beginning. Reaffirming this law he forbade divorce in a sweeping formula that must be authentic, since Matthew, who certainly addressed Jews versed in rabbinical law, also gives it: "What God has joined, let no man put asunder."

Now, this formula is already Gentile-slanted; it is couched in terms of Gentile law. Its word for "man" is not *anēr* (= the male of the race) but *anthropos* (= a man or a woman).

Mark's second formula merely restates that first one:

> Whoever divorces his wife and marries another commits adultery against her; and if she divorces her husband and marries another, she commits adultery (10:11 ff.).

This second formula, therefore, is no more Gentile-slanted than the one it restates, which was certainly addressed to Jews.

We can now sum up the evidence of its design that we have found in the second gospel:

First, its "text" is the record of an apostolic catechesis, probably Peter's, which was given to Jews before 42 A.D.

Second, it was adapted for Gentiles, probably Latin, by equipping it with a modest and inadequate apparatus of notes.

Third, the writer was at pains to reproduce exactly the original catechesis. He omitted nothing, even though the matter, like the unwashed-hands dispute had no interest for Gentiles, or might be hopelessly obscure for them, or even offensive to them — as Jesus' allusion to them as "dogs" (7:27) was. Nor did he add anything that Jesus said which would make them happy; he would not even complete the messianic prophecy with which the gospel opens.

12

THE TWO TRADITIONS

The conclusions we have reached from our analysis of the second gospel agree exactly with the testimony of the early Church tradition; with the official voice of that great confederacy of persecuted, underground churches which had grown up in all regions of the Roman Empire.

The unanimous voice of those churches declared that our second gospel was written by Mark, the disciple and interpreter of Peter. That it was the exact record of the instructions Peter had given him. So exact, that they regarded it as equivalently Peter's gospel. "Peter's memoirs," Justin called it in a writing of the mid-second century.[10] And Tertullian at the beginning of the third century wrote, "they declare it is Peter's gospel, whose interpreter Mark was."[11]

The earliest witness of the tradition is John the Elder, one of "the Lord's disciples" whose testimony is recalled by Papias around 130 A.D.[12] This John the Elder was probably the apostle John; in any case, as a man who had been personally instructed and trained by Jesus, he had been a leader in the Church from the beginning, knew Peter well, and was familiar with the cir-

10. Justin, **Dialogue with Tryphon,** 106.
11. Tertullian, **Adversus Marcionem** 4, 5.
12. The passage from Papias is found in Eusebius, **Ecclesiastical History,** 3, 3, 39.

cumstances in which Peter's interpreter wrote his gospel. This, according to Papias, is what he said:

> Mark, who had been Peter's interpreter, wrote an exact account of all he remembered — not, indeed, systematically — of Christ's words and deeds. For he had not heard the Lord nor followed him, but later, as I said, he followed Peter, who used to give his instructions in a way suited to his listeners, not like a systematic arranger of the Lord's revelations (*logia*). So Mark was not at fault in recording things just as he remembered them; for he had but one object: to leave out nothing he had heard and to make no mistakes.

That whole passage, not merely the first sentence, is the testimony of John the Elder. The one who interjects "as I said" into the second sentence is not Papias; for it was not Papias who had said that Mark followed Peter. It was the Elder who had said so when he said Mark had been Peter's interpreter. And the Elder goes on to explain that (1) Mark recorded the instructions Peter had given him *when he was the apostle's disciple and interpreter;* (2) that this record was exact and complete.

Origen, in the middle of the third century, fastened on those same two points in the tradition. "Mark," he says, "wrote the second gospel *as Peter had instructed him.*"[13]

The next question, then, that we have to ask this tradition is, "*When* was Mark the disciple of Peter?"

It replies, "He was Peter's disciple in Jerusalem."

That testimony is explicitly in the so-called Monarchian prologues of the gospel, dating from the third and fourth centuries. These tell us:

> Mark, God's evangelist and Peter's son by baptism as well as disciple in the word of God, *while exercising the*

13. Quoted in Eusebius, **Ecclesiastical History**, 6, 25.

priesthood in Israel according to the flesh, became con-
verted as a levite to the faith of Christ. He wrote his
gospel in Italy....[14]

That statement of the Church's tradition is free from any
Monarchian bias of the writer. It agrees, moreover, with the
following data found in the Acts and epistles of the New
Testament:

1. In 1 Pet 5:13, Peter tells the churches of Pontus, Galatia,
Cappadocia, Asia, and Bithynia, "The church at Babylon greets
you; and so does my son Mark."

This Mark, who greets those remote churches and is therefore known to all of them, needs no other identification from
Peter than the title, *ho huios mou*. He is *the* Mark — the one
Mark — who is widely known in the Christian churches as Peter's
disciple, taught and baptized by Peter. He must therefore be
the Mark, Peter's disciple and interpreter, who wrote the
second gospel.

But he was not Peter's "interpreter" when First Peter was
written; Sylvanus (5:12) was exercising that role. Apparently
he had no more current connection with the apostle than had
every Christian of the Roman church; for Peter mentions him
after Sylvanus (his current assistant) and *after the Roman
church.* His discipleship and service of Peter, consequently, had
been at some earlier time.

Now, in the early sixties when First Peter was written, Paul,
too, wrote a letter to the Colossians in which he spoke of a
Mark who was assisting him (Col 4:10). This Mark, a Jewish
Christian, is sufficiently identified by calling him "the cousin of
Barnabas." He was, therefore, *the* Mark whose name in the
Christian churches was associated with Barnabas; hence he was
the Mark who had been the assistant of Barnabas in the evan-

14. P. Corssen, **Monarchianische Prologe zu den vier Evangelien:** Texte
und Untersuchungen zur Geschichte der altchristlichen Literatur, 15, p. 9.
(Quoted in Sacrae Theologiae Summa I, (Nicolau y Salaverri), p. 227,
Madrid, 1962.)

gelization of Cyprus (Acts 15:39) and in defence of whom Barnabas had quarreled with Paul. Now, this Mark appears to have had some special connection with Peter in Jerusalem before 42 A.D.

On the night before Peter's execution, when he was miraculously freed from prison and had to flee immediately from Herod Agrippa's dominions, the apostle did not go till he had visited one house in Jerusalem. Only one. It was not the house of James, though he had a message for James. It was the house of Mary, the mother of Mark (Acts 12:12).

This Mark, then, who was in Rome in the early sixties, and had apparently been connected with Peter in the old days at Jerusalem, is almost certainly "my son Mark" who had been instructed by Peter and had served as his interpreter. But if he is, then his instruction and his service had come to an end with Peter's flight in 42. He was so well instructed then that Paul and Barnabas selected him (Acts 12:25) to assist them in their projected missionary expedition.

Thus the evidence furnished by Peter, Paul, Luke, and the tradition of the early Church matches in all details the evidence presented by the second gospel itself. They both tell us that the gospel exactly records Peter's Jerusalem catechesis, and that it was published for Gentile Christians of Italy. Such an agreement can have but one explanation; namely, that what they both affirm is a fact.

The seeming contradiction in the testimony that the first gospel gives about itself can now be easily cleared up. The gospel attests that Matthew wrote it in 42 A.D. It also attests that its author used the narrative we find in the second gospel. The solution of the paradox is that Matthew used the catechesis of Peter that Mark later recorded; he did not use Mark's written record of the catechesis. He did not have to use that written record. Peter's catechesis was as familiar to him and to the other apostles as it was to Mark.

For twelve years, from 30 to 42, the Twelve worked together in Jerusalem as a team. The distribution of doctrinal material among them, we ought to assume, was settled by all of them together in conference. The general contents of Peter's catechesis — the introductory one on which the rest had to build theirs — must have been known to Matthew from the start. As Peter went on giving it month after month, year after year, it inevitably became a stereotype. And as the rest listened to it month after month, year after year, they could not help learning that stereotype by heart. When the same cast have rehearsed and presented the same play for a year, is there any member of the cast who does nut know by heart the parts of all the other members? At the end of twelve years every member of the apostolic team ought to have been able to write Mark's gospel as well as Mark did.

Hence there is no reason why Matthew could not have built his gospel on that stereotype in his memory. Nor is there any reason why he should not have done so, since it had been designed at the start to be the foundation on which the rest was built. Thus the conclusions we have drawn from our study of the first gospel lose none of their force. They too, moreover, like our conclusions about the second gospel, are supported by a powerful tradition.

The unanimous voice of the early churches affirmed that Matthew wrote our first gospel. In fact, that it was the first gospel written. Furthermore, that it was written in Hebrew for Jewish Christians while he was in Judea. Eusebius sums the whole tradition up in these words:

> Matthew, when he had preached the faith to the Hebrews and was about to go forth to teach other nations also, furnished those he was leaving with a composition that seemed to keep him still present to them, by writing a gospel in his native language.[15]

Again the voice of a unanimous tradition agrees with the evidence supplied by the first gospel itself.[16] Again we have a

15. Eusebius, op. cit. 3, 24, 6.
16. Though no early witness contradicts the tradition about our first

phenomenon that can be explained only on the supposition that what both voices affirm is a fact. Our first gospel was written by the apostle Matthew in Palestine.

He wrote it, tradition says, in Hebrew. This was one thing our Greek text could not tell us. It is unable to say whether it is Matthew's original work or a translation. But it can and does say that if it is not the original work, it is a faithful translation. Our line-by-line study of it has exposed a design and a message to which an enormous mass of Matthean innovations contributed. A design and a message that are consistent throughout and evoke all the circumstances that our other sources associate with the writing of the first gospel. Only a faithful translation can stand such a test.

gospel, Irenaeus is ambiguous about the time when Matthew wrote it. He says (**Adversus Haereses,** 3, 1, 2) that it was written "when Peter and Paul in Rome were evangelizing and founding the church." If this means that Matthew did not write before Paul came to Rome in 61 A.D., Irenaeus is mistaken. His testimony, given towards the end of the second century, is contradicted by the far earlier testimony of the Acts of the Apostles, the **Preaching of Peter,** and our first gospel itself.

But Irenaeus may mean something else. Suppose he had written, "Matthew wrote when Peter was evangelizing and founding the Roman church." This would have conformed to the old tradition that Peter went to Rome in 42 A.D. to found the Roman church; it would also conform to the three-fold evidence we have just referred to. But it would not conform to ecclesiastical protocol. Long before Irenaeus wrote, the Roman church was claiming Peter and Paul **as its co-founders,** and, it is probable, already had the custom, which it still maintains, of adding Paul's name to Peter's whenever it speaks of its founder.

Irenaeus, elsewhere in his work, ties the two names together in speaking of the origin of the Roman church. Why? Because, doubtless, of ecclesiastical protocol. For the same reason, then, of church protocol he may have tied Paul's name to Peter's in the passage cited, though he was thinking primarily only of Peter.

PART TWO
TWO SAILED FROM PHILIPPI

1

THE RIOT AT EPHESUS

When did Luke start working on the Acts? This question, which bears closely on the date of the third gospel, is the only one that concerns us now. Not those very different questions: when did he finish or publish the book? We shall try to show that he began working on the Acts in 57 A.D. soon after Paul came to Philippi and found him there.

Our first clue to that date is the account of the riot at Ephesus in Acts 19. More precisely, the clue is the discontinuity in the texture of the narrative that occurs just before the account of the riot.

The discontinuity is not in the narrative itself. In this there is no break anywhere; Luke has carefully tied all its episodes together with links of time and causation that make it flow silkily from start to finish. But in the *texture* of the episodes there is a difference like the difference between the sleek and the scrawny cattle of Pharaoh's dream. The episodes of the first two-thirds of the book are all scrawny; those of the last third are all sleek. This difference arises from their lack or abundance of unessential, purely incidental details.

The scrawny episodes have the minimum idea-content demanded by the narrative; just as the scrawny cattle had the minimum material content needed for subsistence. The minimum idea-content of an episode is that which the readers need to grasp its nature, its causal nexus with the events that precede and follow it, and its *point* — the reason why the writer selected it for inclusion in his story. All the episodes of Luke's story have those three essentials. But the scrawny ones have little or nothing more, whereas the sleek ones have an abundance of merely incidental and circumstantial details. And the scrawny ones herd together, the sleek ones herd together; with a boundary, plain as a fence, dividing them. On this side of the boundary there are no sleek episodes, and on that side there are no scrawny ones. On one side reigns what the economists would call an economy of scarcity, and on the other an economy of affluence or abundance.

Our first task is to prove that those two "economies" exist in the Acts, just as we have described them. The task is lightened by the general recognition that the last nine chapters of the book are a zone of abundance, whose episodes teem with circumstantial details.

Every reader senses that abundance as soon as he has embarked at Philippi with Paul and Luke on the voyage to Jerusalem. Since this is the point where the second "we-section" of the book begins, commentators often ascribe the abundance of detail to Luke's use of a travel journal when he wrote those nine chapters. This explanation seems valid; it may blind us, nevertheless, to the fact that the zone of abundance does not start with the voyage to Jerusalem. It starts with the episode immediately before the voyage; with the riot at Ephesus.

There are five riots or public disturbances in the story of the Acts: at Lystra, Philippi, Thessalonica, Ephesus, and Jerusalem. Each was occasioned by the success of Paul's apostolate; each gave proof of his invincible fortitude. Those two features, we may assume, constituted their basic interest for Luke — his basic motive for including them in his story.

Over and above this basic interest, however, some riots had a special appeal for him. Some had serious personal consequences for Paul, which enhanced his fortitude; in the riot at Lystra he was nearly killed. Some had narrative consequences; they forced a change in Paul's plans. And at two of the riots Luke was either on the spot, or at least in the city when it happened — a circumstance that gave it a special personal interest to him. Each of those special features was a reason for *dilating* on the event by adding an appropriate amount of circumstantial detail. If we grade the riots by their possession of these special merits over and above the basic ones, we get these results:

Lystran: +3. (2 for its extremely grave personal consequences to Paul, 1 for the change in his plans that it compelled: he had to leave the city.)

Philippian: +3. (1 for its serious personal consequences to Paul, 1 for its narrative consequences, and 1 for Luke's presence on the spot.)

Thessalonican: +1. (1 for its narrative consequences.)

Ephesian: 0. (It had *no* personal consequences for Paul, it forced no change in his plans, and Luke was not present.)

Jerusalem: +3. (1 for its personal consequences, 1 for its narrative consequences, and 1 for Luke's presence in Jerusalem when the riot happened.)

The riot at Ephesus, we see, had no special narrative merits at all; whereas the Lystran had +3. We would expect Luke, therefore, to pass briefly over the former, and to dilate on the latter. But what does he do? He gives the riot at Lystra *one* verse; and the riot at Ephesus, eighteen.

Here is his account of the riot at Lystra:

> Some Jews arrived from Antioch and Iconium; and after winning over the crowds, they stoned Paul and dragged him outside the city, thinking that he was dead (Acts 14:18).

He has reduced the event, we see, to its essentials — the inciting speech and the mob action — and described each in the fewest possible words.

This, on the other hand, is what he says of the inconsequential flare-up at Ephesus:

At that time there arose no small commotion about the Way. A silversmith named Demetrius, by making silver shrines of Diana, brought no small gains to his craftsmen. He got these together, along with workmen of like occupation, and said,

"Men, you know that our prosperity depends on this trade; and you see and hear that not only at Ephesus, but almost over the whole province of Asia, this man Paul has persuaded and turned away numbers of people, saying, 'Gods made by human hands are no gods at all.' There is danger not only that our business will be discredited, but also the temple of the great Diana, and the magnificence of her whom all Asia and the world worship will be a thing of the past."

Hearing this, they were filled with wrath and cried, "Great is Diana of the Ephesians!"

So the commotion spread through all the city and by a common impulse the people rushed into the theater, dragging with them the Macedonians, Gaius and Aristarchus, Paul's traveling companions. Paul wanted to go before the people but this disciples would not let him. Some of the Asiarchs also, friends of his, sent to him and begged him not to venture into the theater. Meanwhile the people were shouting, some one thing and some another, for the meeting was in confusion and most of them did not know why they had come together. Some of the crowd called on Alexander, as the Jews had pushed him to the front, and he made a gesture with his hand and was going to speak in their defense. But when they saw he was a Jew, a great shout went up from them and they cried for two hours, "Great is Diana of the Ephesians!"

At last the town clerk calmed them and said, "Men of Ephesus, who in the world does not know that the city of Ephesus is the guardian of the temple of the great Diana, and of the stone that fell from the sky? Since this is undeniable, you must be calm and not do anything reckless. For you have brought these men here, though they have committed no sacrilege nor blasphemy against our goddess. If Demetrius and his fellow craftsmen have a charge to bring against them, there are courts and there are governors; let them take legal action. If you demand something more, it will be dealt with in a lawful assembly. Why, we run the risk of being charged with riot over this day's affair, even though no cause for this commotion exists for which we shall not be able to give an account."

With those words he dismissed the assembly (Acts 19:23-40).

That account could have been as jejune as the Lystran with its inciting speech and mob action reduced to this: "Some silversmiths, whose trade was hurt by Paul's preaching, won over the crowds, and there was a tumult in the city till the town clerk calmed them." On its merits the incident deserved no more than that. On its merits the Lystran riot deserved from Luke the eighteen verses he awarded to the Ephesian. With no regard for their merits he deals the former an economy by scarcity and the latter an economy of abundance.

Though it is now clear that the riot at Ephesus lies within the zone of abundance, we have still to show that the zone *begins* with that riot. Or, in other words, that the episode of the Jewish exorcists at Ephesus, which immediately precedes the riot, lies inside the zone of scarcity. To show this, we shall compare it, since it involves the preternatural, with a preternatural incident that occurs *after* the riot at Ephesus — Paul's revival of the dead boy at Troas.

The narrative merits of the two events seem evenly matched; the revival of the boy is a greater marvel, but the episode at Ephesus was more sensational and consequential. What we look for in each story is its adipose tissue: the unnecessary details.

Here is the story of the exorcists:

> Certain of the itinerant Jewish exorcists attempted to invoke the name of the Lord Jesus over those who had evil spirits in them, saying, "I adjure you by the Jesus whom Paul preaches."
>
> Seven sons of Sceva, a Jewish chief-priest, did this. The evil spirit answered, "Jesus I know and Paul I recognize. But who are you?"
>
> And the possessed man sprang at them and beat them all so violently that they fled stripped and bleeding from the house (Acts 19:13-16).

The only unnecessary detail in that account seems to be the possessed man's *springing* at the exorcists. Of the other details some are needed to make the story credible. Ephesus, a pagan city, had no pagan exorcists; and it is unlikely that resident Jews followed that profession. The writer had therefore to explain that they were *itinerant Jews*. An anecdote of the preternatural that claimed to be true ought to give the reader an opportunity to check the facts himself; the writer gives this opportunity by identifying the exorcists as the sons of Sceva, a chief-priest. The other details are needed to make credible this sequel to the incident:

> This became known to all the Jews and Greeks in Ephesus; awe seized them all, and the name of the Lord Jesus came to be held in honor. And many of those who believed came and openly confessed their practices. And many who had practiced magical arts collected their books and burnt them publicly; they reckoned up the price of them and found the sum to be 50,000 pieces of silver (Acts 19:17-19).

Turning from this story with its one superfluous detail to that of the dead boy's resuscitation, we see how different is its texture. We underline the superfluous details in it:

*On the first day of the week, when we had met for
the breaking of bread,* Paul addressed them, as he was
about to leave the next morning; and he prolonged his
address *till midnight. There were many lamps* in the
upper room where we were assembled. And a young man
named Eutychus, who was sitting at the window, was
overcome with drowsiness; as Paul addressed them *at
great length,* he fell asleep and fell down from the third
story to the ground and was picked up a corpse. Paul
went down and laid himself on him and, *having embraced him,* said, "Do not be upset; his soul is in him."
Then he went up *and broke bread and partook of it;* and
having spoken to them *a good while,* till daybreak, he
departed. And they brought the boy away alive *and were
no little comforted* (20:7-12).

From this comparison of the two stories it is clear that the
earlier one, though it stands out from the grey narrative before
it, lies in the zone of scarcity and is the last episode of that zone.

There remains only to show that the zone of scarcity, which
embraces the first two-thirds of the Acts, has no oasis of abundance. The one likely spot for an oasis is the writer's first "we-
section" in chapter 16: it is often said that Luke availed himself
of a travel journal in writing it. The section consists mainly of a
voyage and the riot at Philippi.

We shall compare the voyage, from Troas to Philippi, with
the later one, over the same route reversed, in chapter 20. On
both voyages Luke was Paul's companion; in this respect they
have equal narrative merit. But the earlier one was a momentous
double first: Luke's first association with the famous apostle, and
Paul's first expedition into Europe. It was made still more
momentous by the vision of the Macedonian that caused Paul to
embark on it. Moreover, the route they took did not have to be
told to the reader when they reversed it on the second voyage.
Thus Luke had many reasons for dwelling on that first voyage
and recounting it in greater detail than the second. But again he
proves unreasonable. Here is his account of the first voyage:

> Sailing from Troas, we ran a straight course to Samothrace, and the next day to Neapolis, and thence to Philippi, the principal city of a part of Macedonia, a Roman colony. We stayed some days in this city (16:11 ff.).

Except for the stops made on the way, those words give us only the essential facts. Luke had to note the importance of Philippi; it explains why Paul stayed there to preach. And he had to note that it was a Roman colony; this explains the charge made against Paul to the magistrates of the city.

Now we look at the account of the reverse voyage in chapter 20, with its load of superfluous details:

> *There accompained him Sopater of Berea, the son of Pyrrhus; and of the Thessalonians Aristarchus and Secundus; Gaius of Derbe, and Timothy; and of the province of Asia, Tychicus and Trophimus. These, having gone in advance, waited for us at Troas*: but we ourselves sailed from Philippi *after the Passover* and *five days later joined them* at Troas, where we stayed *seven days* (20:4-6).

This account, obviously, has an economy of abundance, and the earlier one an economy of scarcity. Furthermore, the contrast between the vague "some days" of the stay in Philippi and the precise "seven days" of the stay in Troas strongly suggests that Luke had no travel journal of the earlier voyage to refer to. The suggestion is confirmed by the brevity and vagueness of his account of the commotion in Philippi. This commotion, we recall, had serious personal consequences for Paul (he was scourged, imprisoned and put in the stocks); it had narrative consequences (he was forced to leave the city); and Luke was on the spot, probably in the market place itself, when the disturbance happened. How brief, nevertheless; how vague and jejune his account is, compared with that of the riot at Ephesus, which had none of those narrative merits!

On seeing their hope of profit gone, her masters seized Paul and Silas, dragged them to the market place to the authorities; and when they had brought them before the magistrates, said,

"These men are Jews and are making a great disturbance in our town. They advocate practices which we Romans are not allowed to adopt or observe."

The crowd joined in the attack on them, and the magistrates had them stripped and scourged... (16:19-23).

Look at that inciting speech. What magistrates would take action on a charge as vague as "making a great disturbance" and "advocating illegal practices"? They would insist on concrete details, even if they did not insist on proofs. And how vague is Luke's account of the mob action; "the crowd joined in the attack on them." He did infinitely better than that with the action at Ephesus, which he had not witnessed.

We conclude, then, that there is no oasis of plenty in chapter 16, and that Luke had no travel journal to refer to in writing it.

We have now established the existence of a discontinuity in the texture of the story of the Acts. Before the riot at Ephesus there is an economy of scarcity; starting with that riot there is an economy of abundance. How is this phenomenon to be explained?

The narrative merit of the episodes does not explain it. For the first two-thirds of the story all the episodes, regardless of their merit, are scrawny; for the last third all, regardless of their merit, are sleek. We have to conclude that Luke, careful of continuity in his story, would have removed that particular discontinuity if he could. He would have given the first two-thirds as rich a texture as the last third, if he could. He was not able to furnish that earlier part of the book with an abundance of circumstantial details, *because he did not know them.* This, of course, shows that his book is strictly factual. Had he been an inventor of details, his story would have no discontinuity of texture; his account of the Lystran riot would have been as vivid and circumstantial as the Ephesian, and his market-place uproar at Philippi as exciting as the temple-court tumult in Jerusalem. We need not, however, labor this point; many another test has proved that Luke's narrative is factual. The question now before us is this: Why was he able to furnish an abundance of details for all the episodes, starting with the riot at Ephesus?

To this question there seems to be only one answer; for that last stretch of the book he was furnished with notes that had been taken while the events were still recent. When an event is still recent we remember its circumstantial details; as it recedes, we forget them.

Who made those notes that Luke used? Luke himself.

They were made, in the first place, as a single note-taking project by a single person. If Luke had used two or more sets of notes (as some suppose he used two travel journals, one of his first voyage with Paul, the other of his second), we would expect to find at least *some* sleek episodes in the first two-thirds of his work, and some scrawny ones in the last third.

Assuming, then, that a single person made the notes as a single project, this person could only be Paul himself or Aristarchus or Luke. He had to be someone who was on the voyage from Caesarea to Italy, because the ship wintered in Malta, and notes of the voyage up to that point had to be recorded in Malta while its recollections were fresh. He had also to be someone who could take notes about the riot at Ephesus while it was still recent. Now, Paul satisfied those two conditions. So did Aristarchus; he had been in the amphitheater at Ephesus when the riot occurred, and he was on the voyage from Caesarea to Rome.

Luke, too, satisfied those conditions. He was with Paul on the voyage to Rome; the apostle's only other companion besides Aristarchus. And he was in Philippi when Paul arrived there with Aristarchus and Gaius less than two weeks after the riot at Ephesus. For Paul had sailed from Ephesus to Troas immediately after the riot. That trip would take, probably, from four to seven days; from Troas to Ephesus took four days. Arrived in Troas, Paul did not tarry there, but reembarked as soon as he could for Philippi — a voyage of three days — and got there with his companions, their vivid memories of the riot undimmed by the eventless journeying since. And there at Philippi, we have just said, they found Luke.

On what grounds do we assert that? Luke's first "we-section" ends in Philippi (16:17), and his second begins there (20:5); but this may be pure coincidence. It does not warrant the inference that Luke was in Philippi for all or part of the seven-years' interval between Acts 16:17 and 20:5.

Our reasons for believing he was in Philippi when Paul returned there in 57 A.D.[1] are these two: he seems to have been the Philippian church's representative, who carried its alms to the needy Christians of Judea; and he seems to have entered Paul's service at Philippi soon after Paul arrived there from Ephesus.

1. He was the Philippian church's representative, and therefore a resident of Philippi. Paul wanted his churches in Macedonia and Achaia to send aid to Judea, and he wanted the aid brought by delegates chosen by those churches. We learn this from 1 Cor 16:3. Since his Macedonian churches gave him both aid and delegates (2 Cor 8:2-5), a representative of the Philippian church went with Paul to Jerusalem. Luke gives us a list of Paul's party on that journey in Acts 20:4. It is Luke's intention, whenever he lists Paul's companions, to omit none of them. That is why in Acts 15:2 he adds the phrase, "and some others," to the name of Barnabas; he wants to make the list complete. That is why, too, in Acts 27:2 he mentions Aristarchus with full identification ("a Macedonian from Thessalonica") although Aristarchus plays no part in the events that follow; he wants

---

1. Paul was brought before Festus as soon as the latter became procurator of Judea (Acts 25:1-12), an event that occured probably in 60 A.D. Paul had then been a prisoner for two years. So he had made his voyage to Jerusalem in 58 and had revisited Philippi in 57.

us to know the whole party that made the voyage to Rome. Now, if the list in 20:4 is complete, except for Luke himself, who is added by implication in 20:5, then Luke was the Philippians' representative, since none of the persons on his list was a Philippian.

2. Luke seems to have entered Paul's service in Philippi. We gather this from a reference to him in Second Corinthians. Paul probably wrote Second Corinthians in Philippi before he moved on to his other Macedonian churches. He wrote it in the flood of emotion released by Titus's arrival with good news from Corinth; and Titus almost certainly came while Paul was still in Philippi, for his visit to the three Macedonian churches lasted at least three months — about a month, then, for each of them — and Titus, coming up from Corinth on a "collision course" to Paul's from Ephesus, and already overdue when Paul reached Troas, could hardly fail to find him at Philippi in the month he spent there.

Now in 2 Cor 8:22 Paul tells the Corinthians that he is sending to them, along with Titus and a "brother" who seems to be Aristarchus, another "brother" who has these characteristics. First, he had proved helpful to Paul in the past. Second, he is *now* much more zealous; in fact, since Paul *sends* him, he now serves Paul as a member of his staff. Third, he is, as 2 Cor 8:23 tells us, a representative of one of the Macedonian churches on the charitable mission to Judea. The only man with those three characteristics was Luke.

He had helped Paul in the past at Philippi. He entered Paul's service, as a permanent member of his staff, some time before he embarked with Paul at Philippi in the spring of 58 to go to Jerusalem; for from that time on he is with Paul, or (when Paul is in prison at Caesarea and Rome) he is close to Paul; he is described by Paul to Philemon as "my co-worker"; that is, as a member of Paul's staff; and he is still with Paul near the end of the apostle's life (2 Tim 4:11). He was also, as we have seen, the Philippians' representative on the charitable mission.

No other man who was with Paul on the voyage to Jerusalem had those three characteristics. Two of the party, Sopater and

Secundus, seem to have been merely the other two representatives of the Macedonian churches — not members of Paul's staff. The remaining six were already members of his staff before he came to Philippi.

Now, if Luke entered Paul's service at Philippi, he not only was able to make all the notes on the events in the Acts starting with the riot at Ephesus; he, and no one else, made them.

Those notes, made in execution of a single project, cover three and a half years; from the summer or autumn of 57 to the spring of 61. To take detailed notes while journeying on foot or in the cramped quarters of an ancient ship was a trying task; to persevere in it for three and a half years needed uncommon tenacity; which, in turn, required strong motivation in the one who undertook the task. What could the strong motivation be? Pleasure or utility or both. There is pleasure, when one sets out on an exciting or momentous voyage, in keeping a travel journal; and there is utility in detailed notes, made while events are fresh, if one is going to write a book about them. But for Paul there could be neither pleasure nor utility in starting a travel journal immediately after the riot at Ephesus. Certainly not pleasure; for the prospect of new journeys could stir none in one who was soon to write of his past travels with such memories as these:

> "Thrice I suffered shipwreck, a night and a day I was adrift on the sea; in journeyings often, in perils from floods, in perils from robbers, in perils from my own nation, in perils from the Gentiles, in perils in the city, in perils in the wilderness, in perils at sea, in perils from false brethren, in labor and hardships, in many sleepless nights, in hunger and thirst, in days without food, in cold and nakedness" (2 Cor 11:25-27).

And what use would Paul have for notes, when he had no leisure to write books?

Aristarchus, too, lacked the strong motivation for starting a series of notes after leaving Ephesus. For him, too, a veteran member of Paul's staff, journeys were no glamorous novelty; and his routine chores, which had left him no leisure for writing books up to then, promised no such leisure in the future.

So Luke made the notes. To him they would be useful in writing a book. And, in fact, he did use them in writing a book.

Soon, then, after Paul came to Philippi in 57, Luke entered his service and started work on a book whose main theme is apparent from the notes of the first incident that he jotted down. It was a book on Paul's apostolate.

Was that book the Acts of the Apostles that he gave us, or some earlier work that has not come down to us, except insofar as he later incorporated matter from it into the Acts? His starting the book in 57, at the same time that he entered Paul's service, furnishes a clue to the answer.

The book was necessarily a part of his service, since it could be written only in the time that he had put at Paul's disposal to aid Paul's apostolic work. Its scope therefore was determined by Paul; it was shaped by Paul's apostolic needs as he saw them in 57 when he came to Philippi. If those needs called for a book exactly corresponding to the Acts, and if the Acts shows no signs of having been adapted to later needs of Paul, then the Acts was the book Luke started to work on in 57.

We shall now try to verify those two Ifs.

2

BATTLES OUTSIDE, FEARS WITHIN

When Paul came to Philippi that year, he was tortured with anxiety. "My flesh had no rest," he wrote. "There was affliction everywhere; battles outside, fears within" (2 Cor 7:2). His battles were fought to save his churches in Achaia and Galatia. His fears were for all his churches, for a common danger, revealed by those battles, threatened all of them, the danger that new preachers would invade them in his absence and seduce his converts from the doctrine he had taught them and from their obedience to his authority. This danger sprang from weaknesses that were inherent in his apostolate. That was why it threatened all his churches.

The weaknesses were two. One was in his claim to be an apostle. An apostle (using that title in its strict sense) was a man who had been personally commissioned by Christ. Christ's commission of the Twelve had been so public that no one questioned it. But Paul had become a Christian after Christ's death and ascension; and he could produce no witness at all to support his claim to be Christ's apostle. Paul pointed to his miracles. these were his credentials; these proved that God himself witnessed to the truth of his claim. And these, together with Paul's apostolic abnegation, produced an overwhelming impression when he preached. But when he had founded a church and moved on, and a year or two had passed, and glib theologians, armed with laudatory letters from older churches, came to urge the fundamental question, "When did Christ ever make Paul his apostle?", even Paul's miracles and sanctity could be thrown into doubt. That was the first weakness a meddlesome innovator could exploit.

The other was the inadequacy of the elders whom he left in charge of his churches when he moved on. These men were new converts, not much better instructed in the faith than those they were supposed to guide and defend; quite unable, therefore, to cope with the arguments and erudition of prestigious preachers from older churches — of whom there seem to have been many in circulation. Fr. Hans Küng has called attention in a recent book (*The Church*) to the insignificance of the elders in all but the late letters of Paul; their inherent weakness as leaders explains the scant notice they receive.

Two revolts, stirred up by intruders in his churches, made Paul see that the threat to his work was general. In each revolt his adversaries had impeached his apostolic authority by contrasting him with the Twelve; and each time the swift spread of the revolt had exposed the inadequacy of the men he had appointed to maintain his doctrine and authority.

The first revolt was in Galatia. Here the intruders were rigorists from Judea, who had informed Paul's converts that he was in error when he taught them they did not have to be circumcised and observe the Mosaic Law. Paul was contradicted by the Twelve on this basic point — and Paul had got his instruction from the Twelve. The celerity with which these meddlers, who had come to Galatia not long after Paul's departure, overthrew his work amazed him:

> I marvel that you are so quickly deserting him who called you to the grace of Christ, changing to another gospel . . . O senseless Galatians, who has bewitched you? . . . I am at a loss what to make of you (Gal 1:6; 3:1; 4:20)!

This revolt may still have been going on when the second one broke out in Corinth.[2] The storm this time blew from the

2. Another theory puts the disturbance in the Galatian churches, and

opposite quarter; these intruders were laxists. "All things are licit to me," was their maxim. They were apostles as much as Paul, they claimed; "sham apostles" *he* called them. They contrasted him disparagingly with the Twelve, the apostles "par excellence," though even these, they asserted, had no right to dictate to mature Christians, "spiritual men."

Their campaign, too, had been swift and successful. When First Corinthians was written, in the spring of 57, Paul was already grappling with the disturbers and believed he had the situation in hand. But before he wrote Second Corinthians six months later, he went through agonies of fear lest his work in Corinth might have been destroyed. He went there on a flying visit from Ephesus; he followed it with a fiery letter, now lost, "written in affliction and anguish, with many tears" (2 Cor 2:4); then, fearing its effect on the Corinthians might be disastrous, he had sent Titus. And when Titus had not reported to him at Troas, he became too restless to stay there and wait for him. "I had no peace of mind ... so, bidding them farewell, I went on to Macedonia" (2 Cor 2:13). And even when he wrote Second Corinthians after Titus had reported that the tide had turned in his favor, some were still in rebellion, and the obedience of most was imperfect, as warnings like these show:

> The weapons of our warfare are not natural ones; they have divine power to demolish strongholds. We destroy arguments and every proud hindrance to the knowledge of God, and take every mind captive to obey Christ, being ready to punish all disobedience when your own obedience is complete (10:4-6).

Paul's letter to them, much earlier — around 48 A.D. While this theory too is probable, adopting it would not weaken the argument here presented, which says that two commotions, arising from widely different doctrinal pretexts in widely distant churches, would indicate to Paul an inherent weakness in, and a general danger to, his apostolic work. As soon as the second of these troubles — the Corinthian — arose, the existence of the danger would become manifest.

When this second disturbance broke out in a quarter so distant from the first and with a doctrinal trend so contrary to it, how could Paul fail to fear for his other churches? The fear was haunting him six months later when he made his gloomy prediction to the Ephesian elders:

> I know that after my departure fierce wolves will get in among you and will not spare the flock. And from yourselves men will arise speaking perverse things (Acts 20:29 ff.).

What else but a general danger that he saw threatening all his churches, once he had left them, could have given him this "knowledge" about a church still in its first fervor?

What defense could he provide against the danger? The best one, evidently, was to put an adequate man in charge of each church — a thoroughly trained member of his staff. This was precisely what he did towards the end of his life when the time for consolidating his work came. But now, when the Spirit kept driving him on ever further, "to the ends of the earth," founding new churches, he could not spare a Timothy or a Titus for each church.

There remained only one other way for him to bolster his churches in his absence. By furnishing them with a book that fully established his authority. A book that vindicated all the claims he had made in his Galatian and Corinthian letters.

What were those claims?

The Galatian innovators had denied his equality with the Twelve. He depended on the Twelve, they said, and was contradicted by the Twelve in his teaching on circumcision.

At Corinth, too, his adversaries had denied him the name of an apostle; at least, in the highest meaning of that title. But they had gone further. Garbling his own doctrine of Christian freedom, they had asserted their independence of all external authority. "You are already full!" he had observed sarcastically. "You are already rich! Without us you are kings!" (1 Cor 4:8). Spiritual men, they contended, men moved by God's Spirit within them, had no use for outside guidance; and their possession of charismatic gifts, such as glossolalia and prophecy, was evidence that the Spirit moved them.

Paul's reply to the innovators in both quarters can be summed up as follows:

1. He defined the role of an apostle, using this title in its highest sense. The apostle is "Christ's minister" and "the man in charge" of God's mysteries; that is, of the whole divine program of salvation in the New Testament (1 Cor 4:1). His role is similar to that of Moses in the Old Testament, but on a far higher plane; he is, like Moses, God's vicegerent teaching and ruling the people of God (2 Cor 3:6-13). As such, he is the visible mouthpiece of God and of Christ, and is clothed with the majesty of their authority; God speaks through him (2 Cor 15:2) and Christ speaks through him (2 Cor 13:2). All members of the Church, therefore — even the "spirituals"— even the prophets — are under his authority:

> If anyone thinks he is a prophet or spiritual, let him recognize that the things I write to you are the Lord's commandments. If anyone ignores this, he shall be ignored (1 Cor 14:36).

2. Paul declares the credentials that an apostle must have to prove he is Christ's and God's spokesman. He must have a personal mandate from Christ (1 Cor 9:1; 15:8 ff.). Furthermore, he must be invested with divine power. To display that power is, in fact, the necessary and sufficient guarantee of his claim to possess a personal mandate from Christ. Such a display of power is the test to which Paul will put his adversaries in Corinth:

> I shall come to you soon, if God wills, and shall learn, not the words of these puffed-up men, but their power. For the kingdom of God is not a thing of words but of power (1 Cor 4:19).

When he himself had preached to them, he reminds the Corinthians, he had shown them divine power:

> My speaking and preaching were not in the persuasive words of human wisdom but in the display of the Spirit and of power.... The signs of the apostle were most patiently displayed when I was among you in miracles and wonders and deeds of power (1 Cor 2:4; 2 Cor 12:11).

He had given the Galatians a like reminder:

> I want to learn from you just this: ... Did he who gave you the Spirit and worked miracles among you, do so from the works of the Law or from your hearing and believing (Gal 3:2-5)?

The Holy Spirit endows the genuine apostle with a second mark: a heroic abnegation, an invincible fortitude (1 Cor 4:9-13; Cor 4:8-12; 6:4-10; 11:23-28).

A third mark, stemming from the displays of power and holiness, is the success of his work — the men he gains to Christ. "*You* are the seal of my apostolate," Paul tells the Corinthians. "You are *my letter* of commendation ... known and read by all men" (1 Cor 9:2; 2 Cor 3:2).

In the passages we have been using to give Paul's ideas about the role, the authority, and the credentials of an apostle, he asserts their fulfillment in himself; yes, even to the height of the Twelve, the apostles "par excellence." Even to the height of Peter himself, the leader of the Twelve; what any man dared in that matter, he dared (2 Cor 11:21; 12:11). His thesis (if we may so call it) is summed up in these lines to the Galatians:

> To me was entrusted the gospel for the Gentiles, as to Peter the gospel for the Jews; since he who worked in Peter for the apostolate of the Jews worked also in me among the Gentiles (Gal 2:7 ff.; cf. 1 Cor 15:10).

The book Paul needed for his churches in 57 A.D. had to prove this thesis to the hilt. The thesis imposed on the book a predictable structure and contents. If that structure and those contents are identical with the structure and contents of the Acts, the Acts was the book Luke started to work on in 57.

What structure did the thesis demand?

The book should be a story in two parts, bound together by a comparison. Its first part would recount the apostolate of the Jews and show God working chiefly in Peter to achieve its success. The second would be devoted to the evangelization of the Gentiles and show God working chiefly in Paul to achieve its success. The bond between the two parts would be the parity of the signs of divine power that had attended Peter and of those that attended Paul.

As for the contents of the book; since the first part would present the standard of apostleship by which Paul was to be measured in the second part, it should depict the role and authority of an apostle emphasizing his divine authority to teach and rule the people of God. It would also define his credentials; in the first place, his mandate from Christ; and then his investiture with power by the Holy Spirit; a power that would display itself in miracles, invincible fortitude, and success. This first part would also stress Peter's leadership in the evangelization of the Jews, making evident, by the preeminence of the miracles attending him, that this leadership was divinely ordained.

The second part would have to prove Paul's mandate from Christ. It would match the divine signs attending his apostolate with those that had attended Peter's. Since the book emanated indirectly from Paul himself, it should not stress, but only hint at, his invincible fortitude. It would, in addition to these general claims, take care of some important ones that Paul had made only with reference to the situation in Galatia, or to the very different one in Corinth.

It is already clear how closely that book Paul needed in 57 resembles the Acts.

The Acts is a two-part story, whose first part reviews the apostolate of the Jews under Peter's leadership; and the second, that of the Gentiles under Paul's. The first part sets the apostolic standard by which Paul will be measured. The apostles rule the and teach the people of God (2:42; 4:34; 6:2-6; 9:27). In that role they are God's vicegerents so immediately that the couple who lied to them, Peter says, have lied to God. Their mandate from Christ is carefully distinguished from their investiture with power. When Christ has given them their commision, he instructs them not to start evangelizing till they "receive power from the Holy Spirit" (1:8). This power is displayed, after they have received it, in many "signs and wonders," which are the main reason for their success (2:43-47; 4:33; 5:12). The invincible fortitude the Spirit has imparted to them is also noted in 5:40-42 and 8:1. Though these credentials are possessed by the Twelve in common, power and success are preeminent in Peter.

Paul enters the book in the first part, where his commission from Christ is narrated. This had been the one vulnerable point in Paul's claims. Luke describes it so skillfully, with its antecedents and consequents, that denial of the commission is made almost impossible. He does not rely on the testimony of Paul's companions, nor of Ananias's, though he does not overlook them. What he highlights is the instantaneous reversal of Paul's breakneck course from full speed ahead to full speed astern; from persecuting to devouring persecutions. *Digitus Dei est hic;* we discern the miraculous here. It is God himself who witnesses to the truth of Paul's commission.

When he has received it, however, he has still to wait several years before he is launched by the Spirit on his apostolate to the Gentiles (13:2); this is the moment when he is clothed with power. Now his miracles begin; and with the first of them Luke starts to show his parity with Peter; he who worked with Peter for the apostolate of the Jews now works with Paul for that of the Gentiles. Peter had used divine power to punish a couple who had "lied to God"; Paul uses it to punish Elymas (13:9). Peter had cured a man born lame; Paul duplicates that miracle in Lystra (14:8). Peter was miraculously released from prison at night; the same happens to Paul at Philippi (16:26). When

Peter preached to Cornelius' party, they spoke in tongues; Paul's preaching has the same effect in Ephesus (19:6). Peter's shadow had been enough to cure the sick on whom it fell; handkerchiefs that have touched Paul do the same (19:12). Peter raised a dead woman to life; Paul raises a dead boy. Peter's successes in Judea are more than matched by those of Paul in Galatia, Macedonia, Achaia, and Asia: "I have labored more than any of them," he tells them in 1 Corinthians 15:10; "not I, of course, but the grace of God with me."

In its general structure and contents, then, the Acts is identical with the book Paul needed in 57. Moreover, it deals as well with certain claims that were peculiar either to the Galatian crisis or to the Corinthian.

He had insisted, against his Galatian detractors, that the Twelve — certainly the chief of the Twelve — had approved his teaching on circumcision (Gal 2:7-9). Luke devotes two chapters of the Acts to the proof of that assertion. He shows his readers not merely the apostles, but also the elders of the Judean church, approving Paul's doctrine and condemning his adversaries (15:24-29).

In Corinth a certain faction had set up Apollos, an eloquent Jewish convert, as a rival to Paul. With great tact Paul, who supported this convert's zealous work, nevertheless indicated the essential difference between their roles by comparing himself to an architect who has laid the foundation of a building, and Apollos to the mason who must build thereon, conforming his work to that of the architect. Luke proceeds with equal tact; he praises Apollos, but adds the shattering detail that he had received his instruction in the faith from two zealous laymen, disciples of Paul (18:24-28).

The identity of the Acts with the book Paul needed in 57 — is therefore complete.

Nor does the Acts betray in its structure or contents any mark of adaptation to a need or utility arising in some later period of Paul's life. Some have believed it was designed to refute Roman accusations that were made against Paul in Nero's persecution; but if that were the case, the whole first part of the book and much of the second would be irrelevant. In fact, any attempt to adapt the book Paul needed in 57 to meet the new needs of 64-68 A.D. would have to subtract from, or add to, its structure or contents. Where is there any sign of such an alteration? To meet adequately the charges made by Roman authorities against Paul in 64-68, the story would have to be brought down to those years. It is not. It is carried just far enough to establish Paul's divine mission to all the Gentiles; to his arrival in the capital of the empire, and the beginning of his preaching there.

We conclude, then, that the Acts was the book Luke started to work on in 57.

3

THE THIRD GOSPEL

We now turn to Luke's gospel. We shall study its design as we studied Matthew's; observing the patterns in Luke's changes of the Petrine catechesis. But the connection of his gospel with the Acts has put in our hands another important tool for the study of its design.

The third gospel and the Acts are two parts of a single plan.[3] This is clear from the way Luke fused them into one continuous story with a single dedication and a single statement of his purpose.

The gospel's opening sentence is a formal dedication:

> Inasmuch as many have essayed to set forth in orderly detail an account of the events that have reached their fulfillment in us, as they were told us by those who from the beginning were eye-witnesses and servants of the Word, I too decided, most excellent Theophilus, to investigate all things minutely from the beginning and give you an exact, step-by-step account, so that you may realize the certainty of the doctrines you were taught.

Luke addresses his patron with a title of honor: *"most excellent* Theophilus." He announces his general subject: the Christian

3. The assertion made by the author of the Acts, that he also wrote our third gospel, stands up under every stylistic test that has been applied to the two works.

story *from its beginning down to its fulfillment among us.* He
states his general purpose: to give Theophilus *certainty about the
doctrines he was taught.* And he indicates the grounds he will
furnish for this certainty: *the accounts of eye-witnesses who
were dedicated servants of the Word* — accounts minutely
checked by Luke.

The opening sentence of the Acts reminds us of that prologue. Again Luke addresses Theophilus. But this time he gives
him no title of honor. Why not? Because this opening sentence
is not a new prologue, but a mere reminder of the prologue of
the gospel — a reminder that Luke is pursuing the same story he
started then. He had engaged to carry the story "from its beginning down to its fulfillment among us." He had brought it only
half-way:

> I wrote the first book, Theophilus, about all that
> Jesus did and taught *from the beginning till the day
> when he was taken up....*

The Acts will carry the story from there down to "its fulfillment among us." Without ending this first sentence Luke starts
splicing the action of his new book to the end action of his
gospel. He goes back over that end action and fills in its gaps
of detail.

In the gospel Christ's ascension seemed to follow at once on
his resurrection. Between the two events, Luke now shows, there
was an interval of forty days:

> ...to whom, moreover, he had shown himself alive
> after his passion by many proofs, appearing to them for
> forty days, and speaking to them about the kingdom of
> God....

Christ's last instruction seems in the gospel to have been
given on Easter Sunday. It runs as folows:

> Thus it is written; and thus the Christ should suffer
> and should rise again from the dead on the third day;

and that repentance and remission of sins should be preached in his name to all the nations, beginning from Jerusalem. And you yourselves are witnesses of these things. And I send forth on you the promise of my Father. Stay in the city till you are clothed with power from above.

The opening sentence of the Acts tells us that Jesus gave this instruction when "he gathered them together." Then, having repeated its conclusion in indirect discourse, Luke proceeds in direct discourse to fill another gap:

> ... he bade them not to leave Jerusalem but to wait for the Father's promised gift, "of which you have heard from me; for John baptized with water, but you shall be baptized in the Holy Spirit not many days hence."

In the sentences that follow (1:6-14), Luke goes on splicing his new action into the gospel's end action, right through the ascension of Christ and the return of the apostles to Jerusalem. Thus he produces a strict continuity in his story, which he thereupon carries to its fulfillment "among *us*": the Gentiles. The purpose of that story, therefore, from the commencement of the gospel to the conclusion of the Acts is the one he had announced at the start: to give Theophilus certainty about the doctrines he had been taught.

Since Paul was the teacher whose authority Luke proves in the Acts, Theophilus must have been a member of one of Paul's churches. He knew that Luke had been before, and was now again, a companion of Paul; that is why Luke did not have to explain to him those sudden shifts, at the "we-sections" of the Acts, from the third person to the first person and back again. Nor does Luke now have to explain the presence of those sections in the first person plural. He had already explained them in his prologue, when he had promised Theophilus an account based on the testimony of eyewitnesses. Since Theophilus knew that Luke had been an eyewitness of some events in his story, he would expect Luke to give his personal testimony when he reached those events.

The purpose of the two books was to give Theophilus certainty about Paul's doctrines. The part of that purpose assigned to the Acts was to prove Paul's *authority* to teach them. The part that fell to the gospel must be to show the agreement of those doctrines with the authentic teachings of Christ. Since Luke was going to use the Petrine catechesis as the basis of his gospel story, he would have to accomplish his purpose, as Matthew had done, by altering the catechesis with insertions, transpositions, and omissions. Such, in general, is the hypothesis we have to test.

But there is a further consideration. Luke's decision to write the second part of his story was made in 57 A.D. It seems a reasonable hypothesis that he conceived his total design *then,* and decided to write the whole story — the gospel together with the Acts. If such be the case, Luke strove in his gospel to show the identity of Christ's teaching with the doctrine of Paul *at the stage to which this doctrine had developed in 57 A.D.;* and our analysis of Luke's changes in the Petrine catechesis should disclose the 57 A.D. theology of Paul, bare of features that appear only at a later period of the apostle's life.

Is this hypothesis worth examining? One difficulty in it — that Luke in 57 could not count on having Mark's gospel to use — we shall deal with later. But, apart from that, was Luke capable in 57 of writing a gospel that would show the Pauline theology of 57 transparent in Christ's own teaching?

The difficulty is that Luke, after briefly working with Paul in 50 or thereabouts,[4] had been away from him, so far as we know, for the next seven years; years whose importance for the development of Paul's theology is measured by the distance,

4. In Acts 18:12-17 Paul appears before the tribunal of Gallio, the proconsul of Achaia. Gallio is known to have been proconsul in 52. Paul had come to Corinth almost eighteen months before he was brought to Gallio's tribunal. And before he came to Corinth he had founded churches in Macedonia, of which the earliest was at Philippi. The latest date, consequently, to which we can assign his first arrival in Philippi with Luke would be 50 A.D.

theologically speaking, between the letters to the Thessalonians and those to the Galatians and Corinthians. Before Luke could write such a gospel as we hypothesize, he had to get a thorough grasp of Paul's current thinking. Where was he to get it? Not alone from those later letters; in the capital matter of Christian faith it was not easy to reconcile Paul's Galatian with his Corinthian position. To the Galatians he had preached freedom; from the Corinthians he demanded obedience. "For him who is moved by the Spirit," he had told the Galatians, "there is no law." And the Corinthian agitators, using that very teaching (but giving to "moved by the Spirit" an equivocal sense) had proclaimed that all things were now licit, and that the "spiritual man" was not subject to external regulation.

To clarify and harmonize the doctrine of the Galatian and Corinthian letters — to pull together his whole teaching on faith — Paul had to write a complete treatise. He did it in his letter to the Romans at the beginning of 58. Did he intend this treatise primarily for the Romans? Perhaps not; addressing it to them may have been merely a pretext, or a literary device for one who found it hard to express himself easily except to a definite group of readers. Certainly, if he wanted to have Luke write the sort of gospel we are imagining, he intended it for Luke. For Luke such a guide to Paul's mind was indispensable.

Written in Corinth amid the still smouldering ashes of the recent revolt, Romans is full of memories of that disturbance. The letter aims to destroy the human pride, the self-assurance and self-sufficiency, that had caused that revolt, and would cause all subsequent revolts in the Church. Its motto could be taken from Second Corinthians: to "demolish every stronghold of argument, every proud obstacle to the knowledge of Christ, and to bring every mind captive to the obedience of Christ."

Paul takes for granted that his reader is familiar with the Galatian and Corinthian letters; this is one objection to the view that he wrote his treatise primarily for the Romans. The big doctrines he expounded in those letters are again his subject. They are the stuff from which his theology of faith is woven;

but he does not repeat the expositions that he previously gave. In treating those doctrines Romans is weak where the earlier letters were strong, and strong where they were weak.

Galatians clearly demonstrated that the Christian, by incorporation into Christ, becomes the true "seed" of Abraham. This demonstration does not reappear in Romans, but new facets of the theme are introduced.

First Corinthians developed the theme of baptismal incorporation, expanding it into a detailed exposition of the Church as the mystical body of Christ. Paul's aim in this exposition was to prove that there had to be external regulation of the Christian's action to maintain the Church's unity. This aim is equally vital to him in Romans, and his instructions in chapters 12 to 15 are based on the Corinthian doctrine of the mystical body; yet he merely alludes to that doctrine in 12:3-8.

Second Corinthians stressed the role of the apostles in the Christian life; Paul's own apostolic role in particular. This role, integral to the theology of faith expounded in Romans, is, nevertheless, merely implied in the new letter.

The fundamental thesis of Romans, announced in its opening and repeated in its closing sentence, is that *faith is an obedience*. He is commissioned, Paul says, by God and Christ to effect "the obedience of faith in all the Gentiles" (1:1; 16:26). If "faith" in that context is to be understood subjectively, the obedience he is commissioned to obtain is "the obedience that is faith." If it is to be understood objectively, "faith" means "the gospel," and obedience is the act by which we embrace the gospel. But a "faith" is embraced by an act of faith; to call this act obedience is deliberately to stress that this special kind of faith is an obedience. The meaning drawn from either sense of "faith" is therefore the same, though the objective sense seems to be the one Paul had in mind. Witness such parallel passages as 10:16 ("not all *obeyed the gospel*") and 16:19 ("your *obedience to the faith* is known everywhere").

This obedience must be given to God, to Christ, and to the apostles. Ultimately to God himself; immediately to God in the person of the Son whom he has sent. We give it to Christ in the baptismal confession that "Jesus is Lord" (10:9). By baptism we become members of his body, and we become subject to him as a woman does to her new husband (7:4). The proof that God wills this obedience to be given to his Son is the *"power in accord with a spirit of sanctification" by which Jesus,* since his resurrection from the dead, *has been shown forth as God's Son.* By power; always power. Power, and the manifestation of the sanctifying Spirit.

This does not yet give us the full picture of the obedience of faith. It has to be given to God and Christ through their human instruments, the apostles. Specifically, the Gentiles are all subject to Paul. This obedience is the Christian's *latreia,* his service of God; it is his sacrifice of praise (12:1); and it does not please God if it is withdrawn from the apostles' control. Paul "administers the gospel so that the sacrifice of the Gentiles may become acceptable, sanctified by the Holy Spirit" (15:16). What is the proof of this divine authority? The same as Christ's own. The proof of power.

> I presume to speak only of what God has wrought through me to win the obedience of the Gentiles by word and deed, by the power of signs and wonders, by the power of God's Spirit (15:18).

Paul divides his subject into two parts. The first (chapters 1 to 4) is introductory. It presents the basic facts that should convince a catechumen to accept baptism; presumably, it represents the elementary instruction, the "milk for infants" that Paul had given the Corinthians (1 Cor 3:1). The main part (chapters 5 to 15) is a profounder treatment, his "solid meat" reserved for the mature Christian who seriously desires to grow in the Christian life "from faith to faith." In both parts Paul takes pains to demolish man's pride, his boasted self-sufficiency.

Salvation through faith in a gospel, he declares at the start of his argument, is accomplished by God's power, not man's power. The "justice" man receives is God's justice, not his own. The only sufficiency of the self-sufficient, autonomous man is a sufficiency for breaking with God, not for returning to him. The wrath of God hangs over him, waiting to unfold on the day of judgment. Paul's more immediate concern is with religious self-sufficiency in the Christian. It is this he chiefly aims at when he proposes the Jews as an object lesson. For there is at bottom no difference between the assurance founded on circumcision and the assurance founded on *charismata;* at bottom each dictates to God its own program of justice and will not accept his. Paul aims at the whole tribe of the self-assured, whether Galatian rigorist or Corinthian laxist, when he presents Abraham's faith as the Christian's model; a faith that does not *earn* justice, but merely has justice *credited* to it by pure favor and mercy of God, inasmuch as it is God's forgiveness of a sinner.

Through faith in Christ, then, man receives God's justice and the Christian life begins, for "the just man lives by faith." What is the nature of this faith, this life? The main part (chapters 5 to 15) of Paul's treatise deals with that question.

Through sin we share in the disobedience of Adam; through faith we share in the obedience of Christ. Sin — faith; each of these states is both a "freedom" and a "slavery."

To throw off God's yoke is to be free; that is obvious enough. What is less obvious to the rebel is that he gains his freedom by enslaving himself to the lawless desires within him; desires whose origin is mainly in his body, the "flesh." Since, as introspection shows, we cannot master all of these desires nor keep them from mastering us, they keep us in an iron bondage to sin, from which only God can rescue us.

This rescuing action cannot be merely exterior to us. It is not enough for God to send his Son in the likeness of sinful flesh, nor to have that Son by his obedience even to death make atonement for our disobedience, nor even to have this atonement proclaimed to us. All this outside action leaves unbroken the iron shackles on our soul. We have to be interiorly changed; a new Spirit must be put into us. This Spirit the Father gives to us when we submit to Christ by faith. It is his own Spirit, and Christ's Spirit. It is their love, and the seal of their love. Our realization that we have it assures us we can master all the desires of the "flesh." We can be truly free. Thus faith, which is obviously enough a state of "enslavement"— to Christ, to God — is also freedom from the bondage of sin.

Paul contrasts sin and faith in both their aspects, as freedom and as slavery, in chapter 6:

> Do you not know that if you yield yourselves to any one as obedient slaves, you are slaves of the one whom you obey; either of sin, which leads to death, or of obedience, which leads to justice? But thanks be to God, that you who were once slaves of sin have become obedient from the heart to the standard of teaching to which you were committed, and having been set free from sin, have become slaves of justice. . . . When you were slaves of sin, you were free in regard to justice. . . . But now that you have been set free from sin and have become slaves of God, the return you get is sanctification and its end, eternal life (6:16-22).

Freedom from the Mosaic Law goes with freedom from the bondage of sin, for the purpose of that law was to make sin's bondsmen realize their state and long for release from it. Hence, for those who were already released the Law did not apply.

This inner freedom that faith brings is not the only reason why it is Good News — *the* Good News — for the human race. Paul points out its other attractions.

Faith and sin are both a "slavery"; but faith is an honorable service to him who is infinitely above us and to whom we owe service by the strongest titles. Sin, on the other hand, is a shameful bondage to our irrational impulses; instead of our riding them, they, with terrible spurs and a bridle of iron, ride us.

Faith gives us "access" to the Father. Through our possession of his Spirit we already initially possess the infinite Love from whom we come, the infinite Good for whom our hearts were made and for whom they incessantly thirst. Thus faith gives us peace and joy. Peace and joy! In fact, these, with "justice," are the very definition of God's reign in us and in human society:

"the kingdom of God . . . is justice and peace and joy in the Holy Spirit" (14:17). To these priceless treasures add *hope;* hope that dares beyond all that a finite mind can conceive. For not only does our possession of the Spirit give us God's own life, and divine sonship in Christ; it also destines us to the goal to which Christ has already arrived: Glory! A glorious immortality for our bodies, and a share with Christ in God's reign over the universe.

The man, on the other hand, who asserts his independence of God, has sundered himself from the one Good that can slake his heart's thirst. His enslavement to egoism and self-will keeps him restless, joyless, hopeless; in a state of death and of liability to the judgment that will doom him to everlasting fetters of shame, restlessness, misery, and despair.

Paul does not allow those melancholy thoughts to dominate his exposition of sin and faith. He starts the exposition in chapter 5 by sounding the glad themes of peace, joy, and hope; and to these he returns in chapter 8, to make them his great message, which rises at the end to a hymn of lyric exultation.

He then devotes three chapters (9 to 11) to the rooting out of religious pride and self-sufficiency — of the self-assurance of those who presume to be "just" by their own standard, not God's. This was the reef on which Paul's own people had been wrecked: "ignoring God's justice and seeking to establish their own, they did not submit to God's justice" (10:3). The ruin that overtook them awaits the Christian who is puffed up with self-assurance. "Do not be proud," Paul warns him, "but fear. If God did not spare the natural branches, he will not spare you" (11:21).

Paul's closing words on this subject sum up the divine and human history of the world:

> Just as you (Gentiles) were once disobedient to God but now have received mercy because of (the Jews') disobedience, so they have now been disobedient that by the mercy shown to you they also may receive mercy. For God has consigned all men to disobedience, that he may have mercy on all (11:30-32).

His anxiety to prevent disunion and factions led him in the next four chapters (12 to 15) to inculcate the same social duties he had taught in chapters 8 and 12-14 of First Corinthians, grounding them, as he had done there, in his doctrine of the Mystical Body — in the subordination of individual functions and charisms to the good of the whole Body, and, in the first place, to the authority of the apostles, whose function corresponded to that of the Head of the Body: "By the grace which has been given to me," he begins, "I say to each of you, let no one rate himself higher than he ought..." (12:3).

The same pervading anxiety to prevent new disturbances like those he had just quelled in Corinth comes out again at the very end:

> I exhort you, brethren, to take note of those who create dissensions and difficulties, in opposition to the doctrine you were taught. Avoid them. For such persons do not serve our Lord Jesus Christ, but their own appetites; and by fine and flattering words they deceive the hearts of simple people. For your obedience is known everywhere, and I rejoice in you; but I would have you wise as to what is good, and guileless as to what is evil; then the God of peace will soon crush Satan under your feet (16:17-20).

This great treatise, which crowned, clarified, and integrated the teaching of the three big letters that preceded it, was exactly what Luke needed if Paul wanted him to write a gospel that would show the agreement of Paul's teaching with Christ's own.

But even when he had a copy of Romans to guide him in using Paul's earlier letters, Luke needed something more. Romans is the most difficult of all Paul's letters. It would raise many questions in Luke's mind; to get the answers to them he must have much time alone with Paul. And the busy apostle had ordinarily little time to give him. Yet, if he really wanted Luke to write the gospel we have supposed and to do it effectively, he would have to create the time required for briefing Luke.

Paul created it. When he set out with his large party for Palestine, he made all the rest go ahead of him and Luke to Troas. Then the two embarked alone at Philippi. For the next five days under the Aegean sun and stars Luke could question him to his heart's content. In those five days, according to our hypothesis, the design of the third gospel was hammered out.

To conclude, then, our hypothesis is this: that Luke, like Matthew, overlaid the primitive Petrine catechesis, which we find in Mark's gospel, with a special design of his own; that this design was to show the agreement between Christ's revelation and the teaching of Paul found in his letters up to and including Romans — most of all in the "big four" to the Galatians, Corinthians, and Romans — but above all in Romans; and that, since the design was hammered out on the voyage from Philippi to Troas, no later doctrine than that of Romans should appear in the third gospel.

This hypothesis we shall now test.

4

CHRIST'S JOURNEY TO JERUSALEM

We begin with the great block of non-Marcan material that Luke thrust into the middle part of his gospel story, the part which covers the events from the close of Christ's Galilean ministry to his arrival in Jerusalem. This non-Marcan block, about nine chapters long (9:51-18:14), replaces a short passage in Mark (9:39-10:12). It starts with the start of Christ's journey to Jerusalem. Luke twice repeats further on (13:22 and 17:11) that Jesus is making this journey; he also reports two sayings of Jesus (13:33-35) which show that Jerusalem is his goal.

This big insertion is, nevertheless, not a journey narrative — not the account of a literal progress from Galilee to Jerusalem. When it starts, Jesus is pushing into Samaria on his way to Judea. At 10:38-42 he reaches the home of Martha and Mary in Bethany, a suburb of Jerusalem. But at 13:31-35 he is back in Galilee, in Herod's jurisdiction. At 17:11-19 when he meets the ten lepers, nine Jewish and one Samaritan, he is again where he was when the journey started: on the border between Galilee and Samaria.

What role, then, does the big insertion play in Luke's design? Is the "journey" nothing but a dumping ground for materials he could not weave into the frame of the Marcan story? Or has it some principle of order? Are the materials united by some symbolic meaning that Luke saw in Christ's journey?

Certainly it is not a dumping ground for otherwise undisposable materials. Luke *transfers* to the journey materials that Mark located elsewhere. For example, Mark — and Matthew too

— put at the beginning of the Galilean ministry Christ's proclamation that "the kingdom of God is at hand" (Mk 1:15; Mt
4:17). Luke moves it to the beginning of the journey (10:11).
Such transferred materials suggest that some principle of order
presides over the contents of his journey narrative.

Why does he suppress in Christ's Galilean ministry the proclamation that the kingdom of God is at hand? Is Luke not
interested in Christ's preaching of the kingdom at that period?
No; he is more interested in it than are Matthew and Mark. He
has five mentions of it that are not in Mark: Lk 4:43; 6:20; 7:28;
9:2; 9:11. Two of these are not found in Matthew either.

Why then does he withhold the proclamation till the start of
the journey to Jerusalem? Some other transfers of material may
throw light on the problem. He moves to the journey *all* the
Matthean texts indicating the imminence of the kingdom, that
Matthew had embedded in the Galilean ministry. It seems, then,
that *Luke wants to link the arrival of the kingdom with Christ's
arrival in Jerusalem.* He moves the Lord's Prayer (with the
petition, "Thy kingdom come") from the sermon on the mount
to Lk 11:2. He also shifts the precept to "seek the kingdom of
God" from the same sermon to Lk 12:31. He moves Christ's
declaration that "the kingdom of heaven (present in its king)
endures violence," from Christ's reply to John in Matthew 11 to
Lk 16:16. And he moves the whole house-divided discourse (in
its Matthean form which contains Christ's proof that "the kingdom of God has come upon you") to Lk 11:20.

His shifting of the text about the violence that assails the
kingdom seems to draw in its wake the shift of *all* the Matthean
texts in which Christ demands of his followers a readiness for
total sacrifice. Those that occur in Matthew 8:18-22 and in
Matthew 10 turn up in Luke 9:57-62; 10:3; 12:2-9; 12:51-53;
14:25-27; and 17:33.

The Jerusalem journey, after these transfers, begins to look
like the process of struggle and sacrifice by which the kingdom
is attained, first by Christ, and then by his followers under and
with him. Jerusalem, the goal of the journey, would symbolize
in that case the kingdom itself.

The shift of the house-divided discourse entails further transfers of Matthean matter. That discourse, pronouncing doom on the Jewish nation, has links with the Matthean temple discourse and passages of the reply to John. As Luke shifts the house-divided discourse to the journey, so he does too with the passages (Mt 11:20-30) that Matthew had annexed to the reply to John. These passages reappear in Luke 10:13-15 and 10:21 ff. Luke does the same with Matthean elements in the temple discourse of Holy Tuesday. The Matthean parable of the marriage feast has its equivalent in that of the great supper (Luke 14:16-24). At the dinner to which a Pharisee invites Jesus in Luke 11 the seven woes turn up. When we study the Lucan version of them side by side with the Matthean, it becomes clear that Luke has taken them from their natural context, which is the one they have in Matthew.

Luke introduces them in this way:

> A Pharisee asked him to dine with him. And he went in and reclined at table. The Pharisee began to ponder and ask himself why he had not washed before dinner. But the Lord said to him:
> "Now you Pharisees clean the outside of the cup and the dish, but within you are full of robbery and wickedness. Fools, did not he who made the outside make the inside too? Still, give the contents as alms, and behold all things are clean to you."

The situation here is similar to the one in Mark and Matthew (Mk 7:1-23 and Mt 15:1-20) where the Pharisees asked Jesus why his disciples ate with unwashed hands, and Jesus replied that what went into a man did not defile him, but what came from him did. That reply had been an effective rebuttal; the one Jesus gives here is not. It begins with the fifth Matthean woe of Holy Tuesday. Jesus asks, "Did not he who made the outside make the inside too?" To which the Pharisee could retort, "Then both should be washed and you have not washed the outside!" Luke, aware of the difficulty, veers off at once to a counsel of almsgiving which further confuses Christ's argument. What is the reason for this confusion? Is it not that Luke has forced the Matthean passage into an improper context?

Consider next these lines aimed at the doctors of the Law, the Scribes:

> Woe to you who build the monuments of the prophets, whom your fathers killed! So you are witnesses and you approve your fathers' deeds; because they killed them and you build (11:47-49).

The logic of this charge is so obscure that we have to clarify it from the parallel passage in Matthew:

> Woe to you, Scribes and Pharisees, hypocrites! You build the sepulchres of the prophets and adorn the tombs of the just, and say, "If we had lived in the days of our fathers, we would not have been their accomplices in the blood of the prophets." Thus you are witnesses against yourselves that you are the sons of those who killed the prophets.

Luke has compressed this magnificent oratory, it seems, in order to make it fit into a dinner conversation, and compression has obscured it.

In Matthew, Christ had continued:

> You, too, fill up the measure of your fathers! Serpents, brood of vipers, how are you to escape the judgment of hell? That is why, lo, I am sending you prophets and wise men and scribes; and some of them you will put to death and crucify; and some you will scourge in your synagogues and persecute from town to town. . . .

Luke, compressing this tremendous climax, again fails to avoid obscurity:

> That is why *the wisdom of God said*: "I will send them prophets and apostles, and some of them they will kill and persecute, that the blood of all the prophets that has been shed from the foundation of the world may be required of this generation. . . ."

Nowhere in Scripture could that oracle of "the wisdom of God" to which Jesus alluded be found; hence it was incomprehensible to his listeners. Luke has made Jesus *quote himself;* Paul in 1 Cor 2:24 calls Christ "the wisdom of God." He is, patiently, forcing the Matthean passage into an unnatural context in pursuance of his design.

In sum, then, *all* the Matthean passages that express Christ's rejection of the Jewish nation and its leaders — whether those passages precede or whether they follow his journey to Jerusalem — are transferred by Luke to the journey. The deliberateness of the transfers is plain; and in the case of some at least, it is also plain that his design is not to put the passages in their true historical context. He has some other reason for making Jesus condemn and cast off Israel as he journeys to Jerusalem. What is this reason? His transfer of the last Matthean element in the temple discourse — the apostrophe to Jerusalem — to the journey seems to throw light on that question.

The apostrophe turns up in Luke 13:34-35. When we study it side by side with the Matthean version in the Matthean context, the difference is evident. In Matthew it is a farewell; in Luke it is a salutation from afar, filled with promise.

In Matthew Jesus says:

> Behold, your house is left to you *empty. For* I say to you, *from now on,* you shall not see me till you say, "Blessed is he who comes in the name of the Lord."

Luke's version omits "empty" and "from now on"; and it replaces "for" by "and."

Behold, your house is left to you. And I say to you, you shall not see me, till you say. . . .

Till Jerusalem says what? What "the whole multitude of Jesus' disciples" will shout with joy as they enter the city on Palm Sunday (Luke 19:38). Jesus speaks to a Jerusalem that is to be redeemed.

From those two passages arise the vista of two cities. From the Matthean, the vista of a Jerusalem doomed and abandoned by Christ. From the Lucan, that of a Jerusalem saved and made the dwelling place of the messianic king, the city that so often in the prophets (Isaias 60-62, for instance) symbolizes the messianic kingdom.

Two Jerusalems. The same two that Paul speaks of in Galatians 4: "the present Jerusalem" (the Jewish nation) and "the Jerusalem from above" (the Church).

Matthew had concentrated his attention on "the present Jerusalem" Luke, it seems, concentrates his on "the Jerusalem from above"; this is what he seems to see at the end of Christ's journey. That hypothesis is further strengthened by some contrasts between Luke's Holy Week story and those of Mark and Matthew.

In Matthew's Palm Sunday story Jesus clashes with his enemies and crushes them after he enters the city and the temple. For this clash Luke substitutes one, equally crushing, that takes place *before* Jesus enters the city. Christ's enemies are not in the procession of his disciples who enter after him. They stand at the side of the road and remain behind, outside. His reply to them is a lightning flash that reveals the cosmic meaning of this moment: "I tell you, if these keep silence, the stones will cry out." This is the moment for which all creation has waited. As Paul will tell the Romans (8:19-22), "all creation yearns and groans for its liberation."

Immediately after this reply Jesus comes in sight of the city, and Luke drops into its place the last Matthean element in Christ's judgment on the Jewish nation. He had already given the equivalent of the Matthean parable of the marriage feast —

except for the picture of Jerusalem's destruction. Now he gives us the equivalent of that picture:

> When he drew near and saw the city, he wept over it, saying, "If thou hadst known, in this thy day, even thou, the things that are for thy peace! But now they are hidden from thy eyes. For days will come on thee when thy enemies will throw up a rampart about thee and surround thee and shut thee in on every side, and dash thee to the ground, and thy children within thee, and will not leave in thee one stone on another, because thou hast not known the time of thy visitation."

Thus Luke completes the Matthean judgment on "the present Jerusalem" just before Christ's entrance into the city, not just before his departure from it. The Matthean departure of Christ is a permanent one; the Lucan entrance inaugurates a *permanent residence*. The king takes possession of his capital. He establishes his government in his palace.

Nowhere is Mark so precise in his indications of time and place as in his Holy Week narrative. Luke dissolves this precision into a vagueness that makes Christ's occupation of the temple appear a fixed state of things, and his teaching of the people, "the whole people," there a fixed practice. Even the eschatological discourse seems to be delivered there. At its close, Luke remarks:

> *During the days* he was teaching in the temple; *during the nights* he would retire to the Mount of Olives; and all the people used to come early to hear him in the temple (22:37 ff.).

This vagueness, it is true, can be harmonized with Mark's precision. But why did he discard that precision? To attain some design. And the design to which all the other Lucan innovations considered in this chapter point is this: he wants the temple where Christ teaches all the people to represent the Church.

"Know you not," Paul tells the Corinthians (1 Cor 3:16), "that you are the temple of God?"

In this preliminary probe of Luke's journey story we have sought to gain an inkling of his design from the patterns that appear in his transfers to the journey of material that Mark and Matthew placed either before or after it. From those patterns we conclude that he presents Christ's journey to Jerusalem less as a history than as a symbol — the symbol of Christ's and the Christian's progress to the messianic kingdom. Since the new, the distinctive feature in this presentation is the progress of the Christian under and with Christ to the kingdom, to describe this progress ought to be his special design for the middle section of his gospel.

If that conclusion is correct, his design for the other parts of the gospel becomes clear.

Since the journey represents the Christian's advance to the kingdom, the Holy Week and Easter events in Jerusalem ought to represent, for the Christian as for Christ, the perfect *attainment* of the kingdom.

What would be the function of the Galilean ministry that precedes the journey? Luke has removed from it all the passages that describe the kingdom as near, as well as all the passages that describe the sacrifices and the struggle which the Christian must embrace to attain it. This section, then — much shorter than the middle one — ought to represent the *beginnings* of the Christian life; it should embody the elementary instruction given to beginners.

If these deductions are correct, Luke's division of his matter corresponds to that of Paul's letter to the Romans, whose first four chapters state the elementary teaching about justification (our entrance into the Christian life), while the bulk of the letter (chapters 5-15) deals with the Christian life as a striving for perfect conformity with Christ, on the principle (Rom 8:17) that "if we suffer with him, we shall also be glorified with him."

Luke's division of his matter would also correspond to Paul's distinction between "milk for infants" (the instruction he gave beginners who were still "carnal"), and the "meat for adults" (which he reserved for the spiritually mature).

Hence, if we have correctly assessed the significance of Luke's innovations in the journey story, all the structural principles of his gospel are derived from the "big four" letters of Paul to the Corinthians, Galatians, and Romans; with Romans as their center and focus. And this result is what the hypothesis developed in the previous chapters of this part of our study led us to expect.

We have still, nonetheless, to verify this result. Do Luke's other innovations in the Galilean ministry support the view that it presents Paul's instruction for Christian beginners? Do his other innovations in the journey story support the view that it presents Paul's instruction for Christians striving to grow in the Christian life? Do his other innovations in the Holy Week-Easter story support the view that it presents Paul's doctrine about the final attainment of the kingdom? Do his innovations remind us of the big four epistles, and most of all, the epistle to the Romans? And, lastly, what function, fitting into such a design, is performed by Luke's infancy story? This final question we shall now take up.

5

JUSTICE, PEACE, AND JOY

In the first sentence of his letter to the Romans Paul had laid down the division of subject matter used by Luke in his two books. The gospel, Paul had said, is "God's Good News about his Son, born of David's line according to the flesh, and shown forth as Son of God by power, joined to a spirit of holiness, consequent on his resurrection from the dead." Luke's gospel starts with Jesus' birth from David's line and carries the story up to his resurrection from the dead. The Acts relates how, consequent on his resurrection from the dead, Jesus was shown forth as Son of God by power, joined to the spirit of holiness that was given to those who believed in him.

Paul had also told the Romans what made that Good News good: "The kingdom of God is *justice and peace and joy in the Holy Spirit*" (Rom 14:17). This definition he had expanded in chapters 5 to 8, which describe the Christian life, and which begin:

> Having been made *just* by faith, let us keep *peace* with God through our Lord Jesus Christ, through whom ... we also *exult* in the hope of the glory of the sons of God ... and *exult* in tribulations too ... and also *exult* in God (5:1-11).

Justice. Peace. And, above all, *joy*: we exult, exult, exult. Joy crowns the other two; it crowns the close of Paul's exposition of the Christian life with a hymn of joy (Rom 8:31-39).

And joy keeps ringing like Christmas bells through Luke's infancy story. Justice and peace are its themes too, but joy crowns them all. We hear it in every incident of the story. In every incident, that is to say, except the last. It is God's own message, brought either by his heavenly messengers, or by his human instruments moved by the Holy Spirit.

Gabriel announces it to Zachary: "Elizabeth will bear thee a son and thou shalt call his name John; and thou shalt have joy and gladness, and many will rejoice at his birth" (1:14).

Joy is his first word to the Virgin; it is the sum of his whole message: "Rejoice," he exclaims, "highly favored one! The Lord is with thee" (1:28)!

When Mary visits her cousin, Elizabeth, "filled with the Holy Spirit," cries ecstatically, "Whence is this that the mother of my Lord comes to me? For at the sound of thy greeting the infant in my womb leaped for joy."

Then Mary, on whom the Holy Spirit has already come, magnifies the Lord: "My spirit *exults* in God my Savior . . . for, behold, from henceforth all generations shall call me blessed."

Zachary, filled with the Holy Spirit, prophesies in that joyous outburst, the *Benedictus.*

To the shepherds on Christmas night the angel brings "tidings of great joy that shall be to you and the whole people." And a multitude of the heavenly army praises God.

Moved by the Holy Spirit, Simeon enters the temple, takes the child in his arms and joyfully exclaims, "Now thou dost dismiss thy servant, Lord, according to thy Word, in peace" (2:29).

In *peace.* Here is that second ingredient of the Good News. In Zachary's song of praise, too, it is the last word: the Rising Sun who is visiting the world "will guide our feet into the way of peace" (1:79). "Peace on earth" to those whom God approves is proclaimed by the angelic host on Christmas night.

The root from which this divine peace and joy spring is *justice.* A justice that is both a total liberation and a total "enslavement"; it is "salvation from the hand of our enemies . . . that, freed from the hand of our enemies, we should serve him without fear in holiness and justice before him all our days" (1:71-75).

Paul had given the Romans another definition of the Good News; it is *"God's power unto salvation to everyone who believes, to the Jew first and to the Greek"* (Rom 1:17).

God's power.

"How shall this be done?" Mary asks the archangel.

"The power of the Most High shall overshadow thee."

By that act of power the child will be recognized as God's Son: "that is why the Holy One born of thee will be called the Son of God."

Thereafter of that act of power Mary says, "He has wrought *might with his arm"*; and Zachary says, "He has raised up *a horn of salvation"*— a mighty saving power —"in the house of David."

This salvation is for everyone who *believes.*

Luke's story starts with two episodes contrasting belief and disbelief in the Good News. Zachary disbelieves and is punished: "Thou shalt be dumb, because thou hast not believed my words, which will be fulfilled in their proper time." Mary believes and is rewarded; "Blessed is she who has believed," says Elizabeth, "that the things promised her by the Lord will be fulfilled."

Salvation to everyone who believes — *to the Jew first.*

Though Zachary has walked blamelessly in the commandments and ordinances of the Lord (1:6), circumcision and the Law have not saved him; he too must hail the Rising Sun who brings redemption, salvation, remission of sins to the children of Abraham. Luke recounts how Jesus was circumcised, was brought to the temple to be offered "according to the prescription of the Law," and went yearly to Jerusalem for the Passover; for, as Paul had told the Galatians, Christ was born "under the Law that he might ransom those who were under the Law" (Gal 4:4).

But salvation was due to the Jews *first,* because God's promises had been given to them and not to the Gentiles. "Christ

Jesus was a minister to the circumcised to show God's fidelity in fulfilling the promises he made to our fathers; but the Gentiles glorify God because of his mercy" (Rom 15:8). Mary, Zachary, and Simeon all sound this theme of God's fidelity, "as he spoke to our fathers, to Abraham and his seed forever" (1:55; 1:70-73; 2:32). The Messias will rule, Gabriel declares, *in the house of Jacob forever.*

But the Gentiles too, Zachary and Simeon prophesy, will be incorporated into this seed of Abraham. He will shine on those who sit in darkness and the shadow of death; he will be a light for the revelation of the Gentiles.

One prophetic word of Simeon's is not joyous. This child who has come for "the ransom of Jerusalem" and for "the consolation of Israel," is set, nevertheless, for the fall as well as for the rise of many in Israel. There will be a fallen and a risen Israel. Two Israels. Two Jerusalems. Antithetical destinies that will be awarded according to the dispositions in men's hearts towards Christ. The self-sufficient will reject him and be rejected; the humble will receive him and be received:

> He has scattered the proud in their self-conceit; he has put down the mighty from their seats and has exalted the humble. He has filled the hungry with good things and has sent the rich away empty.

Here at the beginning of Luke's gospel is the fundamental lesson Paul had tried to impress on the Corinthians.

In the last episode the king who has been announced, who has entered the world but has remained voiceless and passive in the hands of others, speaks. A single word. At the very end of the episode. Luke's whole infancy story has led up to this word. And at this word it stops. It has reached its goal. All his other themes — salvation, liberation, joy, peace, power — are all subordinated to this one. What is this theme to which all his other themes (themes of Paul's letter to the Romans) tend? The central theme of that letter. Christ's obedience. Christ's first word announces it: "Did you not know that I must be in my Father's house?"

"I *must.*"

A divine program has been prepared for him, and he must fulfill it. Of that program he will often speak in the subsequent pages of Luke's gospel; on its last page he will sum it up in these sweeping terms:

> These are the words which I spoke to you while I was yet with you, that *all things must be fulfilled that are written in the Law of Moses and the Prophets and the Psalms concerning me* (24:44).

"I must be *in my Father's house.*"

All that had been written about him had concerned the task he must perform for his Father's house — for that people whom God had chosen to be his dwelling place, whose symbol was the temple of cedar and stone in Jerusalem. He has now begun to give his witness and to teach in it; later he will cleanse and take possession of it. Luke's gospel will end where it began — in the temple.

"Do you not know that *you* are the temple of God?"

The function indicated for Luke's infancy story by this survey is the same as that performed for the first gospel by Matthew's infancy story, that is, it is a prologue announcing the themes and adumbrating the design of the main story that follows it. And the themes announced, the design adumbrated, in Luke's prologue are precisely those required by our hypothesis.

6

MILK FOR INFANTS

Mark's story of Christ's Galilean ministry ends with the dialogue between Jesus and his apostles near Caesarea Philippi. Luke cuts this story short at the first multiplication of loaves; he rearranges its episodes, at the cost of historical exactness; he fails to mention the place where the dialogue occurred. Hence he was not interested in the Galilean ministry primarily as a narrative, but as an exposition — as a teaching. In this new approach lies his special design. According to our hypothesis, he made it an exposition of Paul's instruction for Christian beginners — his "milk for infants."

Luke starts by welding the body of his gospel into a strict continuity with his infancy story:

> And in the fifteenth year of the reign of Tiberius Caesar, when Pontius Pilate was procurator of Judea, and Herod tetrarch of Galilee, and Philip his brother tetrarch of the district of Iturea and Trachonitis, and Lysanias tetrarch of Abilene, in the priesthood of Annas and Caiaphas, the word of God came to John, the son of Zachary, in the desert.

This was the word for which John, who had been in the desert from his early years (1:80), had been waiting.

Luke's precise dating of the event, and his copious details about the rulers of Palestine when it occurred, serve the same purpose as his earlier explanation that imperial census coinciding with Christ's birth was the first one made in Syria by Quirinius. Such details illustrate his care to get the exact facts.

When he repeats Mark's opening quotation from Isaias, he inserts, as we noted when discussing Mark's gospel, the closing words about the conversion of the Gentiles: "All mankind shall see the salvation of God" (3:4-6).

The first episode in the story is John's baptism of Jesus. Its Marcan-Matthean version had these parts: 1. John baptizes the crowds; 2. He preaches, and declares the inferiority of his own baptism to the baptism in the Holy Spirit that will be given by the Mighty One who comes after him; 3. Jesus arrives, and as he is baptized, the Holy Spirit descends and remains on him.

This Marcan-Matthean structure of the episode, with a partition placed between John's baptizing of the crowds and his baptizing of Jesus, sharply distinguishes John's own imperfect baptism from the Christian baptism which was inaugurated at the baptism of Jesus. Luke discards this structure. He replaces it with one in which 1. John preaches; 2. He is arrested; 3. He baptizes *Jesus and "the whole people"* together.

The preaching begins with the warning that John in Matthew had addressed to the Jewish leaders. Luke has him address it to the crowds:

> Brood of vipers! who has shown you how to flee from the wrath to come? Bring forth therefore fruits worthy of repentance. . . .

It is the Jewish *nation* that is threatened with imminent rejection and the sight of God raising up "from these stones" children of Abraham.

The preaching continues with some examples of "worthy fruits"; these are acts of charity and justice. John ends with the announcement of the Mighty One who comes after him and will baptize the people in the Holy Spirit.

The notice of John's arrest (3:19 ff.) interrupts the episode and makes a partition between the preaching of penance and the baptism that follows — a baptism that will embody the Pauline doctrine of Christian baptism. Thus Luke makes prominent, as he will do in the Acts, the preaching of penance that precedes Christian baptism. He will make it the first point in Paul's instruction of beginners (Acts 13:24; 17:30; 21:21); in Acts 26:20 Paul will even insist on "works worthy of repentance."

Luke says nothing of Jesus coming to John. His fusion of the two baptisms — that of "the whole people" with that of Jesus — produces a tableau of the Church:

> It came to pass when the whole people were baptized, Jesus being baptized and praying, that heaven was opened, the Holy Spirit in bodily form like a dove came down on him, and a voice from heaven was heard: "Thou art my beloved Son, in whom I am well pleased."

There we see the whole people brought into solidarity with Jesus through their union with him in baptism. In answer to his mediatorial prayer the Spirit descends on him, and from him is extended to all who have solidarity with him. There is only one Spirit; there is only one Son.

"For in one Spirit," we heard Paul teach the Corinthians, "we were all baptized into one body."

Luke's genealogy and his version of Christ's temptations fill out the meaning of the tableau.

How different is Luke's genealogy of Jesus (3:23-38) from the one given by Matthew! The Matthean descends heavily, freighted with the guilt and punishment of the Jewish nation. The Lucan contemplates, not a nation, but the human race. Abraham and David find no place of honor in it. Like the dove that rested on Jesus in the water with the people around him, it soars. Effortlessly swift, it goes up the generations of men from "Joseph son of Heli son of Matthat son of Levi son of Melchi son of Janne" to "Adam son of God." Thus Jesus brings back to God the whole people and all the past generations that Adam had taken away, and the Corinthian doctrine of the Mystical Body is wedded to the Roman doctrine of the antithetical Adams: "As by the disobedience of one man the multitude were made sinners, so by the obedience of one man the multitude are made just."

Luke's version of Christ's temptations is the same as Matthew's except that he puts in the second place the temptation on the high mountain, and in the last place the one on the pinnacle of the temple. Why does he make this temptation the climax? His closing words may furnish a clue:

> Jesus answered and said to him, "It is said, *Thou shalt not tempt the Lord thy God.*"
> And *having completed the whole temptation,* the devil left him for a while.

Jesus, this Lucan conclusion seems to hint, has affirmed that he is God. When that hint is joined to those furnished by Luke's genealogy and his account of Christ's baptism, they can be summed up in a single line of Paul's:

> Truly God was in Christ reconciling the world to himself (2 Cor 5:19).

Thus Luke has overlaid the episodes that precede the Galilean ministry with the most fundamental of all apostolic — and Pauline — messages: "Repent and be baptized."

His transfers of Marcan and Matthean material from the Galilean ministry to the Jerusalem journey have already been studied. His other innovations in the story of that period start with two episodes that he has enlarged and moved from their Marcan-Matthean context. The result is the highlighting of two other fundamental features of Paul's gospel.

The first episode is Christ's visit to Nazareth. Mark and Matthew put it far on in the Galilean period, after the mission of the Twelve and the discourse in parables. Luke moves it to the front of the story and inserts into it details that make it announce a fundamental point in Paul's preaching, the rejection of the Jews and the election of the Gentiles.

> There were many widows in Israel in the days of Elias when heaven was shut up for three years and six months ... and to none of them was Elias sent, but rather to a widow in Sarepta of Sidon. And there were many lepers in Israel in the time of Eliseus the prophet; and not one of them was cleansed, but only Naaman the Syrian.

We recall the words of Paul to the Jews of Pisidian Antioch in Acts 13:46 and in chapters 9 to 11 of Romans.

The prophecy read to the Nazarenes by Christ, and declared fulfilled in their sight, has its own Pauline echoes.

> The Spirit of the Lord is upon me because he has anointed me. He has sent me to bring good news to the poor, to proclaim *release to the captives* and *sight to the blind*, to *free the oppressed*, to proclaim *the accepted year of the Lord.*

Release for the captive, freedom for the oppressed:

> I see another law in my members warring against the law of my mind and making me captive to the law of sin that is in my members. Unhappy man that I am! Who will free me from the body of this death? Thanks be to God — through Jesus Christ our Lord (Rom 7:23-25).

Light for the blind:

> God, who commanded light to shine out of darkness, has shone in our hearts to illumine them with the knowledge of God's glory, shining on the face of Christ (2 Cor 4:6).

The accepted year of the Lord:

> He says, "In an acceptable time I have heard thee, in
> the day of salvation I have helped thee." Behold, *now* is
> the acceptable time; *now* is the day of salvation (2 Cor
> 6:2)!

Luke's other transferred episode is Christ's call of the first
four apostles (Lk 5:1-11). To the Marcan-Matthean version he
adds the miraculous catch of fish, which is Christ's assurance to
those whom he summons to "catch men," that he will support their
apostolate with divine power.

Power. There, in the first appearance of the apostles on the
stage, Luke evokes Paul's criterion for distinguishing the genuine
apostle of Christ.

The preeminence of Peter in the episode should also be noted.
Christ singles him out among the rest, makes him the leader in
the miraculous catch, and the leader in the future apostolate:

> "Do not be afraid. Henceforth thou shalt catch men."

"Thou." Not "you," as in Mark and Matthew. Luke has begun
to prepare the story of his second book, in which he first relates
Peter's preeminence in the apostolate, that he may later match it
with Paul's, in accordance with Paul's own assertion, that "to
me was entrusted the gospel for the uncircumcised, as to Peter
that for the circumcised" (Gal 2:7).

The rest of the innovations in the Galilean ministry seem
aimed at exposing the ingredients of Pauline faith that are
found, all together, in the Galatian formula (Gal 5:6): "In
Christ Jesus neither circumcision avails nor uncircumcision, but
faith that works through love."

Luke's sermon on the mount reduces the Matthean to that
formula. First, love (6:27-45) — that love of our neighbor, which,
Paul had told the Romans, was "the fulfillment of the Law" (Rom

13:10). Then, the total submission to Christ, which is the root from which this love springs (6:46-49). This submission is obedience; not a hearing of Christ's words merely, but *action* in accord with them; it is a faith that *works*:

> Why do you call me "Lord," and do not practice the things I say? Everyone who comes to me and hears my words and acts on them, I will show you what he is like. He is like a man building a house, who dug deep and laid a foundation on rock.... But he who has heard my words and has not acted on them is like a man who built his house on the ground without a foundation.

Luke's prelude to the sermon consists of four blessings followed by four antithetical woes. These describe the two contrary attitudes presented in the Pauline dictum; that "if you live according to the flesh, you will die; but if by the Spirit you put to death the deeds of the flesh, you will live."

The blessings depict the "spiritual" attitude, governed by the Holy Spirit:

> Blessed are you poor... blessed are you who hunger now... blessed are you who weep now... blessed shall you be when men hate you and ostracize you and insult you and spurn your name as evil because of the Son of Man.

The woes depict the "carnal" attitude, governed by egoism, self-sufficiency, pride:

> Woe to you rich... woe to you who are replete now ... woe to you who laugh now... woe to you when all men speak well of you.

Those contrasted blessings and woes remind us of Paul's ironical contrasting of the Corinthians and himself:

You are replete now! You are rich now! Without us you are kings! . . . We are fools for Christ, you are wise in Christ. We are weak, you are strong. You are in honor, we are without honor. . . .

Christ's reply to John (Lk 7:20-35) points to the intellectual grounds — displays of divine power, and fulfillment of messianic prophecies — that men have for submitting to him. The discourse is practically the same as in Matthew, except that Luke transfers to the Jerusalem journey the two passages that Matthew had annexed to the discourse.

It looks as if Luke used Matthew's gospel in this part of his work. His sermon on the mount is the Matthean, stripped down for adaptation to his own design; and Christ's reply to John is the Matthean, similarly stripped down. Between those two discourses he puts a Matthean miracle (the cure of the centurion's servant) immediately after the sermon on the mount; Matthew, too, had connected it to that sermon. After this miracle Luke places the resuscitation of the widow of Naim's son, and then a mass of miracles (7:21) which ends with the words, "to many who were blind he gave sight." Matthew, too, had introduced the reply to John with the raising of a dead person, a mass of miracles, and the healing of two blind men because Christ would begin his list of miracles with "the blind see," and close it with "the dead rise." If Luke omits the prevision of Jewish persecution in Matthew's tenth chapter, it can be because he is going to describe the persecution later in the Acts.

The raising of the widow of Naim's son shows Jesus for the first time displaying his merciful heart — that divine initiative of love on which Paul lays so much stress: "He loved me and delivered himself up for me (Gal 2:20). "Christ's love urges us" (2 Cor 5:14) to respond with love. The love he showed to one woman soon called forth a response of love from another woman.

A worldly-wise Pharisee has invited Jesus to dinner (Lk 7:36-50). A sinful woman breaks in and sobs at Jesus' feet. He pronounces his verdict on her and his host in these words:

> Many sins are forgiven her because she has loved much; but he to whom little is forgiven loves little.

It is therefore *love for Christ* that remits her sins. Yet it is her faith in Christ, he adds at once, that has saved her. Our sub-mission to Christ must start, or at least end, in love of him. This is another aspect of the "faith that works through love." "If any man does not love the Lord," Paul tells the Corinthians, "let him be anathema" (1 Cor 16:21).

Luke rounds off this episode with a notice (8:1-3) of the many women who followed Jesus and provided for him and his disciples. It recalls the part played in Paul's apostolate by women; no less than eight of them are mentioned at the end of his letter to the Romans.

Luke strips down Christ's parable discourse (8:4-18) till it enforces only one lesson: that faith must be *active;* it must work, it must bear fruit. Omitting Mark's second and third seed parables, he leaves only the parable of the sower, the ensuing dialogue between Christ and his disciples, the explanation of the parable, and the lesson that we must put to use the light we have received. Luke transfers to the end of the discourse the incident that in Mark and Matthew had preceded it.

Into Christ's explanation of the parable of the sower Luke makes two small insertions (italicized below) which show his drift:

> The seed is the word of God. And those by the way-side are they who have heard; then the devil comes and takes away the word from their heart, lest they *believe and* be saved. Those upon the rock are they who, when they have heard, receive the word with joy; these have no root, but *believe* for a while and in time of temptation fall away ... (8:11-13).

The transferred incident at the end of the discourse drives home Luke's point. Jesus is told that his mother and his "brethren" stand outside waiting to see him.

> He answered, "My mother and my brethren are they who hear the word of God *and act on it*" (8:19-21).

Luke ends his account of the Galilean ministry with Christ's feeding of the five thousand men with five loaves and two fishes (9:12-17). From there, cutting out seventy-five verses of Marcan incident, he proceeds at once to the dialogue near Caesarea which leads to the Jerusalem journey.

Why did Luke want the miracle of the loaves to come immediately before that journey?

He has overlaid on the Galilean ministry Paul's doctrine for beginners: the call of the Gentiles, the credentials of an apostle, repentance, baptism, and justification by faith. He also seems to make the miracle of the loaves a symbol of the Eucharist. In Acts 2:42 he calls the eucharistic liturgy "the breaking of bread"; and twice in his Easter story (Lk 24:31 and 35) he notes that the straying disciples recognized Jesus in "the breaking of the bread." Let us hypothesize, then, that he wanted to close his exposition of Paul's elementary doctrine with that of the eucharistic bread, which is the Christian's food on his journey to the kingdom — a journey prefigured long ago in the Israelites' journey to the promised land. At once we recall the passage in First Corinthians where Paul compares those two journeys:

> I would not have you ignorant, brethren, that our fathers were all under the cloud and ... all were baptized unto Moses in the cloud and in the sea. And all ate the same spiritual food, and all drank the same spiritual drink; for they drank from the spiritual rock which followed them, the rock being Christ (10:1-4).

Paul points in that passage to the prefigured elements of his own doctrine for beginners: baptism, the apostolic office

(Moses being God's vicegerent as teacher and ruler), the Eucharist, and the Holy Spirit (the spiritual drink supplied by Christ to those who believed in him). But this equipment for the journey had proved insufficient.

> With many of them God was not pleased, for "they were laid low in the desert." Now all these things came to pass as examples to us ... and they were written for our correction (10:5-11).

To attain his goal the Christian needed more than this elementary doctrine. He must accept harder teachings, solid food.

7

MEAT FOR ADULTS

The many passages, found elsewhere in Matthew and Mark, which Luke incorporates into the Jerusalem journey, have led us to surmise that the journey represents the Christian's progress to the kingdom of God, his growth in the life of the Spirit; and that the contents of this section of the gospel present Paul's advanced teachings as they are found in the big four epistles — above all, in Romans, where the Christian's progress is described as the doing to death of egoism in all its forms. We shall now see whether the other material in this section of Luke's work confirms our surmise.

The Marcan prelude to the journey (Mk 8:27-9:39) was so apt for the design we suppose Luke to have had, that he made only minor changes in it — some omissions and a few brief insertions. The prelude began with the revelation, given at Caesarea Philippi, that Jesus *"must* suffer" (here is the consummation of that program of obedience which had been laid down for him) . . . "be rejected . . . be put to death . . . and on the third day rise again."

Then Jesus insists that all who wanted to arrive at that glorious destination must go the same road as he; "If anyone wills to come after me, let him deny himself and take up his cross and follow me."

Into that stern precept Luke inserts one word; the Christian must take up his cross *daily* and follow his Master. It is the program of Christian *living,* and not merely of Christian dying. It is the Pauline program in Romans (also in Galatians 5:24).

In the account of the transfiguration the Lucan insertions underline three points. First, it is Christ's "glory" that the apostles behold: "They saw his glory." Second, that this glory is shared by Moses and Elias — thus recalling Paul's dictum, "If we suffer with him, we shall be glorified with him" (Rom 8:17). Third, Jerusalem is the place where Christ' glory is to be attained: "Moses and Elias, appearing in glory, spoke about his depar-ture, which he was going to *complete in Jerusalem*" (9:31). Jerusalem, as we have already observed, is a key word, and a key symbol of the third gospel.

The whole message of the journey can be read on Christ's face as he begins it:

> When the days for his being taken up were nearing their close, he set his face firmly to go to Jerusalem (9:51).

In that face of the leader appear singleness of purpose and inflexible resolution. But, Luke hastens to tell us in his next episode, Christ's inflexibility was combined with gentleness towards those who opposed him (9:52-56).

Christ then demands the same single-mindedness and resolution of his disciples in a Matthean passage (Lk 9:57-62 = Mt 8:18-22). It is the first illustration of the theme of total renunciation. The theme will reappear in 12:3-9, in 12:51-53, and in 14:25-27. Those are all Matthean passages, but Luke caps the last one with two strong illustrations of his own:

> Which of you, wishing to build a tower, does not sit down first and reckon the necessary costs to see whether he has the means to complete it? ... Or what king, setting out to do battle with another king, does not sit down first to see whether he can with ten thousand men oppose him who comes against him with twenty thousand?

So every one of you who does not renounce all that he possesses cannot be my disciple. Salt is good; but if the salt itself becomes insipid, what is there to salt it with? ... He who has ears to hear, let him hear (14:28-35)!

The mission of the seventy-two disciples (10:1-24) is mentioned only by Luke, but it is built up almost entirely from passages that Matthew had appropriated to the mission of the apostles. In fact, Luke's build-up of the episode makes it overshadow his earlier account (9:1-6) of the mission of the Twelve. He makes the seventy-two share the apostolic office, at least for the duration of their mission. Christ appoints and sends (*apostellei*) them; he clothes them with authority and backs them with miraculous power; when they return, he describes (in a Lucan passage, 10:18-20) the greatness of their achievement and their reward:

> I saw Satan fall like lightning from heaven. Behold, I have given you power to tread on serpents and scorpions, and on all the might of the enemy; and nothing shall hurt you. But do not rejoice in this, that the spirits are subject to you; rejoice rather in this, that your names are written in heaven.

Why does Luke insert this sketch of the apostolic office, so much fuller than the one in Christ's Galilean ministry, into the Jerusalem journey? To make the apostolic office a necessary part of the Christian life in its maturity as well as in its inception. This was the point so strenuously maintained against the Corinthian agitators by Paul, and reaffirmed in his letter to the Romans.

The next theme to appear is the "perfect way" that Paul taught in 1 Corinthians 13, which ended with the words:

> So there remain faith, hope, and charity, these three; but the greatest of them is charity.

Luke expounds the three in 10:25-11:13.
The first and greatest is love.

> "Master, what must I do to attain eternal life?" "Thou
> shalt love the Lord thy God with thy whole heart and
> with thy whole soul and with thy whole strength and with
> thy whole mind, and thy neighbor as thyself."

This teaching is illustrated by the story of the good Samaritan
(10:30-37). It is followed by the anecdote about Martha and
Mary (10:38-40), which contrasts faith with works.

> Mary, having sat down beside the Lord at his feet,
> was listening to his words.

This is an image of Pauline faith: total adhesion to Christ,
total surrender to his words. And this, Christ tells Martha, is
"the one thing necessary."

In the next incident (11:1-13) Jesus teaches his disciples a
shortened form of the Our Father. Then he explains to them, in
a Lucan illustration followed by a Matthean passage from the
sermon on the mount (Mt 7:11), the importance of persisting
in prayer. By changing a single word in the Matthean passage,
Luke gives the Pauline ground for the Christian's *hope*:

> "If you," Christ says, "know how to give good things
> to your children, how much more will your heavenly
> Father give *the Holy Spirit* to those who ask him?"
> "Our hope," Paul will tell the Romans (5:5), "does
> not let us down, because God's love is poured into our
> hearts by the Holy Spirit that he gives to us."

The first part of the house-divided discourse (11:14-26) ends
with the fable of the unclean spirit that has been cast out of a
man and returns with seven worse spirits than itself. This en-

forces the need for steadfastness after conversion — for a face set firmly to Jerusalem. The lesson is driven home in this Lucan incident:

> A woman from the crowd exclaimed, "Blessed is the womb that bore thee, and the breasts that fed thee!"
> He said, "Rather, blessed are they who hear the word of God *and keep it*" (11:27 ff.)!

The rest of the house-divided discourse is, as in Matthew, a condemnation of "this generation." One effect of such transferred Matthean passages has been noted in an earlier chapter; they make the rejection of the Jewish nation take place on Christ's way to the heavenly Jerusalem. But they also serve, like Romans 9 to 11, as a warning to the Gentile Christians against pride and self-sufficiency.

In Luke 13:1-9 the evangelist adds to the Matthean passages that warn the Jews of imminent judgment, a demand for repentance illustrated by the parable of the barren fig tree. The demand did not apply merely to the Jews; Christians too could need repentance — as the Corinthians did (2 Cor. 7:8-11).

The Lucan episode following this parable (13:10-17) recounts the cure of a woman whose back was so bent by an evil spirit that she could not look up at all. Luke seems to see in her a figure of the Gentiles, since he explains the episode by the Matthean parables of the mustard seed and the leaven, which follow at once:

> He said *therefore,* "What is the kingdom of God like? . . . Like a grain of mustard seed.

In the story of the bent woman's cure the Gentiles could glory only in God's merciful initiative. Utterly unable to look up, she was able only to respond to Christ's call:

> He called her to him and said to her, "Woman thou art freed from thy malady." He laid his hands on her, and at once she was made upright and glorified God.

To have a single-minded gaze, an intention purified of all egoism, must be the Christian's first goal. Christ describes it as our guiding light:

> If thy eye be right, thy whole body will be lit; but if it be wrong, thy body will be in darkness. Beware, then, that the light inside thee be not darkness!

The intellectual light inside us guides all our actions to their supreme goal. Any "darkness" in it tends to pervert all our activities. Paul is fond of that contrast between the inner light and darkness: "Let us lay aside the works of darkness," he tells the Romans, "and put on the armor of light" (13:11).

The two forms of egoism Paul fought hardest to dispel from the Corinthians were pride (displayed in self-conceit and self-sufficiency), and covetousness, shown in their reluctance to help the needy Christians of Judea.[5] These two are also the forms of "darkness" that the Lucan Christ most strenuously inveighs against.

It is the Pharisees, of course, who are his chief object-lessons in pride. His judgments on them are given in transferred Matthean passages, but in some purely Lucan ones as well. Two of these, in particular, recall the passages in which Paul warns the Romans not to imitate Jewish self-assurance and self-sufficiency. There is question in both passages of "justification." In

---

5. Paul never mentions the word "covetousness" to the Corinthians. It is, nevertheless, the vice he fights in two whole chapters (8 and 9) of Second Corinthians. Compared to the Macedonians, he tells them, they had an abundance of goods; but they had contributed so meagerly to the collection that he sends Macedonians to shame them into generosity, "lest our boasting about you be found empty," and "we, not to say yourselves, be put to shame" (2 Cor 9:3).

the first (16:14 ff.) Christ tells the Pharisees, assured of their justice, that their pride is an abomination in God's eyes.

In the other passage (18:9-14) the Pharisee and the publican symbolize the two contrasted "justices" that Paul will compare in Romans. The Pharisee's is man's justice, earned by his works. The publican's is God's justice, credited to the sinner who throws himself on God's mercy. It is the publican who is "justified."

Covetousness appears as Christ's theme after the first stricture on Pharisaic pride.

> He said to them, "Take heed and guard yourselves against all covetousness; for a man's life does not consist in the abundance of his possessions" (12:13-15).

Then he tells the story of the rich fool (12:16-21) and goes on to teach detachment from material goods in a Matthean passage from the sermon on the mount. The passage ends with the precept of singlemindedness:

> Seek the kingdom of God, and all these things will be given to you besides (12:31).

Luke recurs over and over to the importance of alms-giving. He had forced this theme, as we have seen, into Christ's lecture to the Pharisees at the dinner table. It is restated more sweepingly in 12:32:

> Do not be afraid, little flock, for it has pleased your Father to give you the kingdom. *Sell what you have, and give alms.*

We meet the theme again at another dinner given by a Pharisee (14:12-14), in the parable of the wasteful steward (16:1-13), and in that of the rich man and Lazarus (16: 19-31).

Christ's lesson in the parable of the wasteful steward was particularly apropos to the collection Paul was making for the

Judean church in 57 A.D. The friends won by the steward through his foresight in diverting his lord's property repaid him handsomely in his need. Christ applies this lesson:

> Make friends for yourselves with the iniquitous mammon, so that when it fails, *they may receive you into the eternal tabernacles.*

These friends can obtain heavenly dwellings for us because they are God's friends and have influence with him. Paul urges this point on the Corinthians when he is stirring them to generosity. The fervent Christians of Judea, he says, can repay them handsomely:

> Your (material) abundance can supply their want, and their (spiritual) abundance can, in its turn, make up what you lack. . . .
> The demonstration you furnish by this service makes them glorify God . . . while *they, in their prayers for you, yearn for you* (2 Cor 8:14; 9:13).

To watch for Christ's return is one of the most emphasized precepts of the New Testament. Constantly recurring in Paul's letters, it rises with him to an intense longing for that return. "*Maranatha!* (Lord, come!)" he exclaims at the end of First Corinthians. All creation, he tells the Romans (8:19-23), shares this longing.

In Matthew and Mark this theme of watching appears only in the eschatological discourse. It occurs there in Luke; but he also puts it twice into the Jerusalem journey, at 12:35-48, and at 17:20-18:8. On this second appearance it becomes an intense longing for Christ's return:

> The days will come when you will long to see one day of the Son of Man, and will not see it.

After this prediction Christ describes his return — it will come like lightning — then, insisting that "they must always pray and not lose heart," he relates this parable:

> There was a judge in a certain town who neither feared God nor respected men. There was a widow in that town who kept coming to him, saying, "Do me justice against my adversary." And for a long time he would not. But afterwards he said within himself, "Though I do not fear God nor respect men, yet because this widow is a nuisance to me, I will do her justice before she wears me out with her continual coming."
> And the Lord said, "Hear what the unjust judge says. And will not God avenge his elect, who cry to him night and day? And will he be slow to act in their cause? I tell you he will avenge them quickly. Yet when the Son of Man comes, do you think he will find faith on earth?"

Other future themes of St. Paul besides that of longing are woven into this picture of Christ's widowed Bride: Paul's insistence on continual prayer (1 Thess 5:16), and the "apostasy" (2 Thess 2:3) that will precede Christ's return.

The strongest motive Paul uses to buoy the Christian and spur him on is found in the contemplation of God's love, made incarnate in Christ:

> God proves his love for us by this, that when we were yet sinners, Christ died for us. Much more now that we are made just by his blood, shall we be saved through him from the wrath (Rom 5:5-10).

The parables in Luke's fifteenth chapter are moving pictures of this love. The first two, the lost sheep and the lost drachma, depict God's initiative and how he prizes the lost one. The parable of the prodigal son reveals the love that impels him.

Since these parables are Christ's reply to the Pharisees who criticized him for consorting with sinners, they identify the Father's initiative and love with his own. At the end of the journey, when Christ brings Zaccheus to a joyous conversion, he will make the point of those parables explicit, saying, "The Son of Man has come to seek and to save what was lost" (19:10).

Into chapters 16 and 17 Luke packs some brief precepts.

In 1 Corinthians 7:10 ff. Paul had to remind his readers that Christ forbade divorce. Luke records the prohibition in 16:18:

> Everyone who divorces his wife and marries another commits adultery; and he who marries a woman who has been divorced by her husband commits adultery.

Paul had written forcefully against the vice of scandal in 1 Corinthians 8:1-15 and 10:14-33; and in Romans 14:1-15:6. Luke inserts a warning against scandal in 17:1 ff.

Next Jesus commands us to show a forgiving spirit (17:3 ff.), as does Paul in Romans 12:17-21.

The familiar Pauline theme of apostolic power reappears when the apostles ask Jesus to increase their faith and he reminds them of the miraculous power that is attached to their office:

> If you have faith like a mustard seed, you would say to this mulberry tree, "Be uprooted and be planted in the sea," and it would obey you" (17:5 ff.).

The comparison with a mustard seed recalls, as it does in Matthew 17:19, the parable of the mustard seed, whose lesson was the divine power that will make the kingdom of God grow and spread.

The vice of spiritual self-complacency which Paul hammers at so often in First Corinthians and in Romans is attacked by Luke once more in 17:7-10, where Christ reminds the Christian of his nothingness as a creature:

> Does (a master) thank his slave for doing what he commanded him? I think not. So do you too, when you have done everything that was commanded you, say, "We are unprofitable servants; we have done what it was our duty to do."

To St. Paul thankfulness towards God is an essential part of the Christian life; he tells the Thessalonians that it should be continual:

> In all things give thanks; for this is the will of God in Christ Jesus regarding you all (1 Thess 5:18).

The Lucan episode of the ten lepers drives home the lesson that gratitude to God is an essential component of the faith that saves:

> He fell on his face giving thanks; and he was a Samaritan. Jesus answered, "Were not the ten made clean? Where are the nine?" ... And he said to him, "Arise, go thy way; *thy faith has saved thee*" (17:11-19).

At Jericho, with the end of the journey in sight, Jesus heals a blind man. Matthew and Mark make the miracle happen when Jesus leaves Jericho. Luke says it took place "on Jesus' approach" to Jericho. Does he contradict the other two evangelists? Possibly; but it is more likely that he has, to suit his design, created the mere semblance of a contradiction. He loosens the joints of his narrative and stretches his syntax pretty far when he likes.

He uses the infinitive construction, "on Jesus' doing something," to signify either simultaneity of action, or immediate sequence: either "while he was doing it," or "after he had done it." When he says in 8:40 that "on Jesus' crossing (the lake), the crowd welcomed him," he describes a welcome that came after the crossing. So, when he says that Jesus cured the blind man "on approaching Jericho," he may be speaking of a cure that took place *after* he had approached the town. Immediately after. But "immediately after" can mean "the day after." Jesus, Luke is going to tell us, entered Jerusalem and cleansed the temple immediately after — viz., on the following day.

Why should Luke put the cure of the blind man before Jesus' entry into Jericho? Because of the two Lucan episodes, the conversion of Zaccheus and the parable of the high-born man, that follow it. These two ought to come *just before Christ enters Jerusalem* because they explain his purpose in coming. This coming, they explain, is for the "departure that he was to complete in Jerusalem.

The departure was, first of all, his death; and this was for the saving of sinners. The words that close the episode of Zaccheus reveal that motive: "The Son of Man has come to seek and to save what was lost."

The departure was also Christ's achievement of his "glory"— his kingdom. And this aspect of it is explained in the parable of the high-born man who goes away to a far country to obtain a kingdom.

Now, if the cure of the blind man ought to precede these two episodes, and the conversion of Zaccheus took place *in* Jericho, Luke either had to say (with Mark and Matthew) that it took place after Jesus left the town, and then, with a clumsy backward jump, continue, "By the way, while Jesus was in Jericho. . . ." Or he had to put the incident where he does. Luke does not like clumsy backward jumps. He eliminates the one that occurs when Mark and Matthew go back to describe the Baptist's death, and the one they make in their story of Peter's three denials of Christ. He has probably loosened his syntax, therefore, to eliminate a third one in his anecdote of the blind man at Jericho.

This alteration in Mark's account seems, then, to be due to Luke's taste as a story-teller — to his personality, not to his design. Leaving it aside, we see that the other Lucan innovations in the journey section — both those we studied in an earlier chapter and those we have just finished with — confirm the hypothesis that he made this section the repository for St. Paul's instructions on growth in the Christian life, particularly as they are found in the big four epistles, and most of all in Romans.

8

BEGINNING FROM JERUSALEM

Luke's account of Christ's passion and resurrection ought, according to our hypothesis, to convey Paul's teaching about the consummation of the Christian's progress under and with Christ to the kingdom; and it should do this by his alterations of the Marcan-Matthean account.

He makes three changes in Christ's reply to the Sadducees on Holy Tuesday. According to Mark, Christ says of the resurrection:

> When they rise from the dead, they neither marry nor are given in marriage, but are like angels in heaven (Mk 12:25).

Here is Luke's version:

> Those *who shall be accounted worthy of that world* neither marry nor take wives. *For neither shall they be able to die any more,* for they are equal to the angels *and are sons of God, being sons of the resurrection* (20:35 ff.).

The first two insertions restrict, as does Paul in 1 Cor 15:50, a glorious resurrection to those who have served the Spirit, and not the "flesh."

> I tell you this, brethren, that flesh and blood cannot attain the kingdom of God, nor can corruption attain incorruption.

The third insertion identifies our full sonship of God with the state we shall reach at the glorious resurrection — a Roman doctrine:

> We who have the first-fruits of the Spirit — we, too, groan within ourselves, *waiting for the adoption as sons, the redemption of our body* (Rom 8:23).

In the eschatological discourse, apart from the material he transferred to his journey story, Luke made two notable changes. In the first he describes the fall of Jerusalem. The signal for the flight of his followers that Jesus gives in the Marcan-Matthean version is the "abomination of desolation which was spoken of by Daniel the prophet"; they were to ponder the prophet's words, and when events showed that their fulfillment was inevitable, the Christians must flee at once. Since they were to disregard earlier, fallacious signs, this signal was to be an unmistakable one. Unless, however, one joined those passages of Daniel (9:27; 11:30-36; 12:11) to Christ's Palm Sunday prophecy when he came in sight of Jerusalem (Lk 19:42-44), they gave no light at all. That Palm Sunday prophecy is, therefore, a necessary antecedent to the eschatological discourse.

The version Luke gives of the signal for flight omits Christ's instruction to read Daniel, and the term, "abomination of desolation," uncouth to the Greek ear as well as unintelligible. Instead he culls some details from Daniel, which the Palm Sunday prophecy showed were pertinent: that a king, who ruled the empire to which the Jews were subject, would send his armies against it, and capture it and desecrate its sanctuary; that many Jews would perish by the sword and flame or be led away captive; but that the Gentile domination of the city would end at the predestined time:

When you see Jerusalem surrounded by an army, then know that her desolation is at hand.... For these are days of vengeance, that all things written may be fulfilled. ...And they will fall by the edge of the sword and be led captive into all lands, and Jerusalem will be trodden down by the Gentiles till the times of the Gentiles are fulfilled (21:20-24).

This first big change in the Marcan version of the discourse seems explicable, therefore, by motives of style. The other change reiterates a Pauline theme which we have met earlier — that of the Christian's yearning for Christ's return: "When these things happen, look up, lift up your heads..." (21:28).

Luke's innovations in the story of the Last Supper shape an image of the Mystical Body, related to the Eucharist, as it appears in First Corinthians: "We, though many, are all one body because we all eat the one body" (1 Cor 10:17).

The Marcan-Matthean version contained four events in this order: 1. Jesus predicts his betrayal. 2. He institutes the Eucharist. 3. He promises to go before them into Galilee after his resurrection. 4. He predicts Peter's three denials of him.

Of those four events Luke left only the last unchanged. He transferred the first, omitted the second, altered the third, and made a number of insertions. Let us begin with his version of the third, the institution of the Eucharist.

Here is the Marcan-Matthean version:

While they were eating, Jesus took bread, and blessing it, he broke and gave it to them, saying, "Take it; this is my body."

And taking a cup and giving thanks he gave it to them, and they all drank of it; and he said to them, "This is my blood of the covenant, which is poured out for many. *Amen I say to you, I will drink no more of the fruit of the vine, till that day when I shall drink it anew in the kingdom of God.*"

That italicized last sentence is put by Luke *before* the words of institution. The effect of the transfer is reinforced by a similar statement of Christ at the beginning of the supper:

> He said to them, "Intensely have I yearned to eat this pasch with you before I suffer; for I say to you that I will eat it no more till it has been fulfilled in the kingdom of God."
>
> And having taken a cup he gave thanks and said, "Take this and share it among you; for I say to you, I will not drink of the fruit of the vine till the kingdom of God come."

After this preliminary cup Jesus institutes the Eucharist and again drinks "the fruit of the vine." At that moment, then, in Luke's version, the kingdom of God comes. The Church. The Mystical Body is present.

The Mystical Body, Paul noted in his Corinthian letters, had traitors among its members. By putting the prediction of betrayal *after* the institution of the Eucharist Luke made Judas a partaker of Christ's body.

Paul had also stressed in his Corinthian letters the need of humility in those who aspired to lead the Church. Luke inserts the episode of the ambitious apostles (probably condensed and transferred from Mark 10:35-45), in order to enforce that need for humility (22:24-27).

Paul had further stressed in those letters his authority, equivalently Christ's own. Luke follows the lesson of humility with his strongest text for the permanence of apostolic rule over the Church:

> You are they who have stayed with me in my trials. And I appoint to you, as my Father appointed to me, a kingdom, that you may eat and drink at my table in my kingdom; and you shall sit on thrones, ruling the twelve tribes of Israel (22:28-30).

Peter receives a special office:

> Simon, Simon, behold, Satan has desired to have *you*
> (all of you) that he may sift you like wheat; but I have
> prayed for *thee* that thy faith may not fail, and thou, once
> converted, strengthen thy brethren (22:31 ff.).

Beyond the role (barely hinted at in 24:34) that Peter may
have played in rallying the other apostles on Easter Sunday, Luke
seems in that passage to be looking ahead to his second book, and
to those moments, decisive for Paul's apostolate, when Peter,
"once converted" after his experience at Joppa, had rallied the
other apostles to the revolutionary policy of admitting the Gentiles into the Church without circumcision.

After the prediction of Peter's three denials comes this last
insertion:

> He said to them, "When I sent you forth without purse
> or wallet or sandals, did you lack anything?"
> They said, "Nothing."
> He said to them, "But now, let him who has a purse
> take it, and likewise a wallet; and let him who has no
> sword sell his shirt and buy one. For I say to you that
> this which is written must yet be fulfilled in me. . . ."

Now that "must" of the divine program sends Christ away,
widowing his Church. A time of struggle has arrived for her;
and the Christian, as Paul warns the Thessalonians and Romans
(1 Thess 5:8; Rom 13:12), must arm himself for the conflict.

Except for the innovations he introduced into the account
of Jesus' trial before the Sanhedrin — innovations due, probably,
to his ideas of how a story should be told[6]— Luke's changes in

6. Luke's innovations appear to spring from his desire to eliminate the
backward leap of the Marcan-Matthean account when it comes to Peter's
denials. The narrative has to divide and go for a while on two roads when

the passion narrative seem designed to present Christ as the motive for the Christian's love and the model for the Christian's imitation.

Love of the Father and of men has left no place in Christ's heart for egoism. He cannot think of himself even in the most frightful suffering and pressure; and he never loses his self-control, or his boundless liberty of spirit. Such are the inferences we draw from his restoration of the severed ear of Malchus, his words to the women of Jerusalem as he drags the cross to Calvary, his prayer for his executioners while they nail him, and his promise to the repentant thief. Perhaps it is another facet of his freedom of spirit that Luke wanted to display when he inserted the story of Christ's appearance before Herod, and the unruffled silence he maintained under the monarch's frivolous questioning and the guffaws of his courtiers.

But Luke also showed his readers how that freedom of spirit had been won — in the dark struggle ("agony" in Greek means *struggle*) when Jesus had sweated blood and prayed all the more intensely and had to be strengthened by an angel.

His resurrection story is dominated by the episode of the two errant disciples. He assigns it 24 verses (24:13-35), whereas

it reaches the high priest's house, where Jesus is led inside and Peter remains in the patio. Whichever road the narrator took, he had to go back and retravel the other — unless he adopted Luke's device. Luke follows Peter up to the third denial, which took place at cock-crow; **from that point on,** he follows Jesus. Hence, he has omitted several hours in Jesus' story — the whole interval between his entering the house and the second crowing of the cock. What had happened during that interval? The trial. Luke has to supply us with this information as he goes on with Jesus' story. He does so as he ushers Jesus into the presence of the Sanhedrin at daybreak:

> They led him away into their Sanhedrin, **saying,** "If you are the Christ, tell us."

He then summarizes the trial that had taken place during the night hours that he had omitted. **"They led him in, saying . . ."** can be a loose way of describing the state of the case as it stood when Jesus was led in.

the apparition of Christ to the Eleven gets only 14, and the ascension only 4. Moreover, he modifies the Marcan account to make it introduce the episode.

His crucial change in the Marcan account is that of the angel's message to the women at the tomb. The angel does *not* remind them of Christ's promise to see his disciples in Galilee. He reminds them of the program of obedience to which Christ had been subject:

> Remember how he spoke to you while he was yet in Galilee, saying that the Son of Man must be betrayed into the hands of sinful men and be crucified and on the third day rise (24:6).

This program becomes the subject on which Christ enlightens the two disciples on the way to Emmaus:

> "Did not the Messias *have* to suffer all these things before he entered his glory?" And beginning with Moses and all the prophets, he explained to them all the Scriptures referring to himself.

They catch fire:

> Did not our hearts burn within us while he spoke with us on the road and explained to us the Scriptures?

And they hurry back to Jerusalem. There Jesus shows himself to the Eleven. His message, once he has proved the reality of his risen body, is that same divine program of obedience:

> These are the words I spoke to you while I was yet with you, that all things *must* be fulfilled which are written in the Law of Moses and the Prophets and the Psalms concerning me.

Now he opened their minds, too, to make them see this program broadening out to all men and bringing them salvation when they embraced it: "Repentance and remission of sins should be preached in his name to all the nations, beginning from Jerusalem."

In embracing this program they themselves found joy:

> They worshiped him and returned to Jerusalem with great joy. And they were continually in the temple, praising God. Amen.

Thus Luke's resurrection story replies to his infancy story. Episodes of joy at the beginning pointed to Christ's obedience. The review of his obedience at the end led to the Christian's joy. There, in that marriage of joy and surrender to Christ, is the central theme of the third gospel. It was also, we recall, the central theme of the letter to the Romans.

Another phrase of Christ in those closing lines should be noted. His gospel, he says, is to be preached to all the nations "beginning from Jerusalem." That phrase recalls another in Paul's great letter.

> "I do not presume to speak," Paul will tell the Romans, "of anything except of what Christ has wrought through me to win the obedience of the Gentiles ... by the power of signs and wonders, by the power of the Holy Spirit, so that *from Jerusalem* as far round as Illyricum I have fully preached the gospel of Christ."

In what sense had Paul's evangelization started from Jerusalem? Only in the sense that the grace fountaining up from Christ's death and resurrection there made it the capital of the kingdom of God, the starting point of all salvation, the Jerusalem from above — our mother.

9

PAUL'S GOSPEL

We have now completed our survey of the third gospel. The patterns that appear in its Lucan innovations are those of Paul's doctrine in the epistles up to and including Romans; they are dominated by the doctrine of Romans. They are the patterns, that is to say, of the Pauline theology of 57 A.D. There is no trace in the gospel of the new attitude to growth in the Christian life that Paul begins to emphasize in the letters to the Colossians and Ephesians, which he wrote at Rome between 61 and 63. In Romans and the earlier letters he had envisaged growth in the Christian life as almost exclusively an ascesis: a growth in self-denial. In the epistles of the captivity he thinks of it much more in terms of contemplation, as a growing in the knowledge of the unsearchable riches of Christ. The third gospel — and, in particular, the journey section, which deals with growth in the Christian life — emphasizes only the ascetical themes of Romans and the earlier epistles.

So the hypothesis about the third gospel that we set out to test has been confirmed. We can conclude, with fair probability it seems, that the work Luke projected and commenced in 57 was the combined work, Gospel and Acts, that he eventually gave us. How long did it take him to finish them?

Since he undertook the work to serve Paul and to relieve a pressing need of Paul's churches, it seems unthinkable that he left its completion till after Paul's death. It seems unthinkable that Paul, whom he served, would permit him to do so. He finished his task, we may be sure, as quickly as he could. What, when we get down to concrete details, does that mean?

His second book, the Acts, should have been well started before Luke sailed for Palestine in 58. He had begun in Philippi to gather the materials for it. All the eye-witnesses for Paul's third expedition were there in Philippi: Timothy, Erastus, Aristarchus, and Gaius. What about the second expedition? Paul had started it with Silas, had picked up Timothy at Lystra, and Luke himself for a while at Troas: from Troas he had gone on to found churches at Philippi, Thessalonica, Berea, Athens, and Corinth. We do not know whether Luke could now reach Silas; but Timothy was with him; in Philippi, moreover, there were plenty of eyewitnesses besides Luke himself of what had happened there. Then, on his way to Corinth, Luke stopped at Thessalonica and Berea, meeting eyewitnesses of Paul's activities there. Either on the way to Corinth, or by an easy side-trip from that town, he could visit Athens. And he was three months in Corinth before he set out with Paul for Palestine. He had gathered in those three months all the material he needed for Acts 16 to 19. Since his task was urgent and he had the leisure to write, he may well have written those four chapters before he left Corinth.

Acts 20 to 28 are pure journalism. From the jottings he made of events as they occurred, he could easily add those chapters to his book — chapters 20 to 24 during the time of Paul's imprisonment before the arrival of Festus; 25 and 26 after Paul's appearance before Agrippa and Festus, while Paul waited for a ship that would take them to Rome; 27 and 28, except for the last two verses, soon after Paul reached Rome. Those last two verses had to wait two more years till it became certain that Paul's imprisonment would end in freedom and not in death.

So much for Acts 16 to 28. What of the first fifteen chapters?

For the events of the first missionary expedition and for some earlier facts in Paul's story Luke needed Barnabas. We know from 1 Cor 9:6 that Barnabas was alive in 57 and that Paul knew where he was; probably still in Cyprus (Acts 15:39). Cyprus is not far from the Palestinian coast; Luke could easily make the short voyage to it during his two years in Palestine.

He could also request and get Barnabas' testimony by letter. At least by letter, too, he could reach Mark; though Mark may even have been home again in Jerusalem when Luke arrived there in the summer of 58.

In Palestine that summer there must still have been an abundance of eyewitnesses, "dedicated servants of the Word," who could tell Luke what Jesus had said and done, and of the events recorded in Acts 1 to 12.

Among those witnesses were the "brothers of the Lord," (they were still alive in 57, as we learn from 1 Cor 9:6); one of them, James, was the leader of the Judean church.

Since most of the "more than five hundred brethren" to whom Christ had appeared were still alive in 57 (1 Cor 15:6), the same should be true of the hundred and twenty disciples who had witnessed the ascension of Jesus and stayed together thereafter till Pentecost. Of those hundred and twenty, upwards of sixty should still be alive in 58. If only half of these were still in Palestine, there were at least thirty eyewitnesses, whose testimony covered the events from the baptism of Jesus onwards, whom Luke could easily reach in his two years in Palestine. They were all leaders of their respective Christian communities, all personally known to the elders in Jerusalem, and all, starting with those elders, cherishing a strong good-will and gratitude to Luke. Paul had seen to this by having Luke carry the generous aid of the Philippians to the needy Christians of Judea. Luke would have their full cooperation in his task of gathering and checking the data he needed for the gospel and the early chapters of the Acts.

Those witnesses could give him not only their own recollections. They could also direct him to written accounts, which they could certify to be those of eyewitnesses. Among such written accounts the most important were Matthew's gospel[7] and the "text" of Peter's Jerusalem catechesis, as recorded by Mark.

7. It is widely believed today that Luke did not know Matthew's gospel. The belief rests on the fact that Luke omits, rearranges, or adapts much Matthean matter. But, as we have often had occasion to repeat in this book, omissions, rearrangements, and adaptations merely prove a difference of

Though Mark may not have published this "text" with "notes" explaining it for the Romans before the sixties, he must have recorded it long before Luke came to Palestine. The vivid, incidental details that cling to the incidents in that "text" are not such as stay in the memory many years after they have been heard. Mark must have written them down not long after Peter's flight from Judea in 42. He must have had that record in his possession when Luke undertook to write a gospel; and Luke could obtain it by reaching Mark.

Writing the third gospel, then, should not have been for Luke either a long or a very difficult task. Mark's gospel furnished its frame and a fourth of its contents. Matthew gave him another fourth. He had only to gather some 550 verses more; for Acts 1 to 15 some 560 more. In his two years in Palestine he should have had little trouble gathering them, and little trouble writing his gospel. When we recall why he undertook the work, and who wanted it finished, we shall be prone to conclude that it was completed before he embarked for Rome with Paul. We shall be even more prone to do so when we remember that the work bears no trace of the new development in Paul's theology that Paul began to emphasize in Rome.

What does the tradition of the early Church report about the third gospel? In the first place, it affirms, unanimously and categorically, that it is "Paul's gospel." Irenaeus writes, "Luke set down in his book the gospel that Paul was preaching."[8] Tertullian says, "Luke's gospel is affirmed to be Paul's."[9] Origen calls Luke's "the gospel that was approved by Paul."[10]

---

design. Do Luke's omissions, rearrangements, and adaptations of Marcan matter prove he was ignorant of Mark's gospel? Not only is Luke's ignorance of Matthew not proved; we have seen many places where he seems to have querried Matthew. Furthermore, his use of Matthew's method of conveying a message by overlaying it on the Petrine catechesis, his use, too, of an infancy story to serve as a prologue, and of a genealogy, are grounds for suspecting that he had given careful study to our first gospel.

8. **Adversus Haereses**, 3, 1, 1.
9. **Adversus Marcionem**, 4, 5.
10. Quoted in Eusebius, **Historia Ecclesiastica**, 6, 25.

In the second place, Eusebius and Jerome, fourth-century writers of vast erudition, inform us that the Church's tradition assigned the writing of the third gospel to an early period in the relations between Luke and Paul. "They say," Eusebius tells us, "that Paul usually referred to Luke's gospel whenever, making mention of his own gospel, he writes, 'according to my gospel.' "[11] The earliest use of that phrase by Paul is in Romans 2:16.

"Luke," Jerome tells us, "wrote the gospel about which Paul says, 'We have sent with him the brother whose praise in the gospel is (heard) in all the churches.' "[12] That quotation from Paul is found in Second Corinthians.

Though our study of Luke's gospel has demonstrated that it could not have been in existence when Paul wrote Second Corinthians and Romans, this tradition connecting it with those epistles is significant because it assigns the gospel to so early a date. Moreover, a connection between the gospel and those two epistles has already been noted in our study. Luke, we have seen, appears to have decided to write it (together with the Acts) at Philippi when Paul was dictating Second Corinthians. And Romans may well have been written to guide Luke in his work.[13]

11. Historia Ecclesiastica, 3, 4.
12. De Scriptoribus Ecclesiasticis, 7.
13. The text we have quoted above from Irenaeus deserves some discussion, because of an ambiguity in it that makes it the favorite patristic text — yes, the one valid patristic text — for scripture scholars who want late dates for the synoptic gospels. Since the ambiguity occurs in the sentence preceding the one we have quoted, we give the whole passage:

> Matthew in the country of the Hebrews . . . produced an account of the gospel when Peter and Paul were evangelizing and founding the church in Rome. After their **exodon,** Mark, the disciple and interpreter of Peter, himself gave us in writing what Peter was preaching (**ta hypo Petrou keryssomena**). Luke too, the follower of Paul, put the gospel he was preaching (**ta hyp' ekeinou keryssomenon evangelion**) into a book.

There was also a tradition, though a meager one, about where the gospel was written. In Achaia, it said. Since this tradition is not contradicted, it is not unlikely that there was some link between the work and Achaia. There may have been more than one link. Theophilus, the patron who disseminated the book, may have lived there. Moreover, as we have seen, the first chapters of Luke's combined work may have been composed in Corinth. A work begun in Achaia may easily, after some generations, be reported as a work written in Achaia.

It is, however, not such thin voices of tradition that interest us; it is tradition's strong, unanimous chorus. And this declares that Luke wrote his gospel during Paul's lifetime with Paul's approval; and that he wrote it before he went to Rome with Paul. With such corroboration the conclusions we have drawn from our study of the book itself can hardly be dismissed as unsupported conjecture.

The present participles, **keryssomena** and **keryssomenon,** express time contemporaneous with the main verb; hence we translate them "was preaching." That is the rule with the present participle, unless the context compels us to give it a past sense. According to the scripture scholars to whom we have just referred, the context does compel us to give those two participles a past sense. For, they say, **exodon** means "decease." If Peter and Paul were already dead when Luke wrote, and if Luke's gospel followed Mark's, then Peter was no longer preaching when Mark wrote, nor Paul when Luke wrote.

But does **exodon** mean "decease"? **Exodos** means "departure" at least as often as it means "decease"; and "departure" is just as natural a sense for it as "decease" in the passage under discussion. It can mean: (1) "After the departure of **Matthew, Peter, and Paul from the country of the Hebrews,** Mark wrote the gospel Peter was preaching. Luke, too, wrote the gospel Paul was preaching." Or it can mean: (2) "When Peter and Paul were absent **from Rome** (on some missionary expedition or a tour of the churches) Mark wrote the gospel Peter was preaching. Luke, too, etc."

We should also note that Eusebius and Jerome, men of vast erudition, who had read the works of Irenaeus that are lost to us, and, of course, were familiar with the passage we are discussing, did not think that **exodon** meant "decease." For they knew of only one tradition about Mark — that he wrote his gospel when Peter was alive — and only one tradition about Luke — that he wrote his when Paul was alive.

Monaghan, Forbes J

    Reflections on the synoptic gospels, and their special design
[by] Forbes J. Monaghan.   Staten Island, N.Y., Alba House
[1970]

xvii, 204 p. 22 cm. 4.95

Includes bibliographical references.

1. Synoptic problem.   I. Title.

BS2555.5.M65   226'.06'6   70-110595
ISBN 0-8189-0171-3   MARC

Library of Congress   70